COME TO THE TABLE

COME TO THE TABLE

A Celebration
of Family Life

Doris Christopher

Warner Books

A Time Warner Company

Warner Books, Inc., 1271 Avenue of the Americas, New York, NY 10020

Visit our Web site at www.twbookmark.com

W . A Time Warner Company

Printed in the United States of America

First Printing: November 1999

10   9   8   7   6   5   4   3   2   1

Library of Congress Cataloging-in-Publication Data

Christopher, Doris
Come to the table : a celebration of family life / Doris Christopher.
       p.   cm.
     ISBN 0-446-52428-X
     1. Food habits—United States—Psychological aspects. 2. Din-
ners and dining—United States—Psychological aspects. 3. Family—
United States. 4. Communication in the family—United States. I.
Title.
GT2853.U5   C57   1999
394.1'2—dc21

                                                              99-26604
                                                                   CIP

Illustrations by Michael Storrings

Book design by James Sinclair

This book is dedicated to my husband, Jay, and to our daughters, Julie and Kelley, in honor of the memorable meals we have shared as a family. And to our parents, Jane and Edward Kelley, and Maxine and Walter Christopher, whose steadfast commitment to family was what first brought us to the table.

Acknowledgments

Bringing a meal to the table often takes the work of many hands. It is no different creating a book. The work of many hands, minds, and hearts are the key ingredients in *Come to the Table*.

Sincere and profound thanks go to Nancy Shulins, whose dedication to this project never wavered. It was wonderful to collaborate with you, Nancy.

Thanks to all of you who shared your family mealtime memories and traditions in the pages of this book. I believe your reflections will inspire families around the world to create and celebrate their own mealtime traditions.

A special thanks also goes to a wonderful group of people who came to the table to help me with this project: Thanks to everyone at Warner Books: to Diana Baroni for you and your team's belief in *Come to the Table* and for your keen eye and sure hand in the editing process; to Jamie Raab for supporting our efforts all the way; and to Heather Fain, Diane Luger, Karen Torres, Elizabeth Hurley, Harvey-Jane Kowal, Thom Whatley, Stacey Ashton, Chris Barba, Julie Saltman, and all who worked to make this book a reality. A special salute to the Linda Chester Literary Agency: to Joanna Pulcini for your infectious enthusiasm and nurturing of this project, to Gary Jaffe for your energy and support and, of course, Linda Chester, for your vision and encouragement. Thanks to our team at The Pampered Chef, Ltd.: to Jane

Edwards, vice president of communications and consumer affairs, a sincere thank you to you and your team for your creativity, leadership, and vision. And to our Kitchen Consultants who help busy home cooks make mealtimes quick, easy, and fun: You are an inspiration to me!

Contents

⋙⋘

COME TO
THE TABLE

Introduction

Some people preserve memories in quilts made from scraps of old baby clothes, others in snapshots they paste into scrapbooks. I store mine in oak at one end of my kitchen, perched on a pedestal and surrounded by chairs. The table: when I look at it, I see my life.

I see my ninety-year-old grandmother in her farmhouse kitchen following a recipe that exists on no page, mixing unmeasured ingredients for the sugar cookies I'll never quite manage to duplicate. I see my mother rushing to the sink in the kitchen of my girlhood, a hissing pressure cooker in her outstretched hands. I see velvety raspberries still warm from the sun on the table of our Michigan cottage.

I see all this and more as I look at my table, my own private home movie coming to life in my mind's eye. Endless images project on the screen of my mind: my two older sisters bending over their homework, my father savoring stew on a cold winter night. The reel turns slowly at first as my parents and siblings give way to my husband and daughters, my mother's gray Formica to my golden oak. I'm a girl, then a teenager, a young wife and mother, and then a mother whose girls have grown up.

Fashions and foods change along with the faces. Mother's pot roast morphs into my lighter, healthier tenderloin, her Southern fried chicken into my low-fat boneless chicken breasts. But other things don't change with the generations. For instance, like my mother and grandmother, I still come to the table to connect with the people I love.

Round or square, mahogany or oak, the table is the heart of every home, the nucleus of domestic life, where we pay bills and wrap presents, fold laundry and toss mail. When the chores are done and daylight is fading, the work table becomes the dinner table, and as we gather around it, we, too, are transformed. No longer separate and solitary, we regain our identities as part of a much greater whole: We become a family, sharing not just our suppers but also ourselves.

It is here, at the table, that we rejoin the pack, in a timeless ritual. Surrounded by the people who matter, gazing into the faces we love, we count our blessings and share our burdens, reliving the daily dramas of missed buses and skinned knees. We raise jelly glasses and champagne flutes, toasting accomplishments in classrooms and boardrooms. And over homemade casseroles or haute cuisine, relatives become loved ones and acquaintances become friends.

The table is where we mark milestones, divulge dreams, bury hatchets, make deals, give thanks, plan vacations, and tell jokes. It's also where children learn the lessons that families teach: manners, cooperation, communication, self-control, values. Following directions. Sitting still. Taking turns. It's where we make up and make merry. It's where we live, between bites.

Some families today have lost sight of the table and its timeless ability to transform. Rather than focus on one another, they gather around the television. It saddens me to think of all the thoughts gone unspoken, the achievements uncelebrated, the lessons unlearned. When I look at my table I think back to all the late nights I spent sitting in my bathrobe, listening to my daughters' accounts of their dates; reading the Sunday paper and discussing world affairs over coffee; bolstering shaky egos or soothing small hurts, salving the wounds that accompany growing up. I recall the countless joys and sorrows, the laughter and tears that come with being part of a family.

Some of my happiest memories at the table don't involve dinner at all, like helping my children with their homework, wrapping Christmas gifts, playing board games or bridge. It isn't to say that the meals aren't important; after all, they're what most often bring us together. Some have been memorable, some not. But either way, it's the coming together, the sharing, that matters most, be it for fast food or the fanciest feast.

Needless to say, life today moves at a much faster pace than it did in my grandmother's day. Like most women today, I'm a juggler of family, home fires, and career. Maintaining a healthy balance is hard at times, and like most women, I don't always succeed. I've come to see it as a lifelong challenge, a fact of life, pure and simple. We all struggle to bring our lives back into balance, only to watch ourselves lose it again. But each day brings a new chance to start over, a new opportunity to reconnect.

Much of what I know about keeping my balance I learned from my own working mother, Jane Kelley. With three daughters, a husband, and a full-time job, she still managed to cook us all dinner, a nightly triumph of efficiency and organization. She was the original make-ahead cook, forming meatballs today for tomorrow's spaghetti, browning Monday's beef for Tuesday's Swiss steak. More hearty than elaborate, her recipes were nonetheless delicious. And these meals accomplished one important thing—they brought us to the table for dinner as a family.

We ate most of our meals in the kitchen, on chrome chairs pulled up to the table in our modest Oak Lawn, Illinois, home. As an auto mechanic with his own service station, our father, Ted, put in long days and was unable to eat with us on weekdays. During my last couple of years of living at home, we always ate supper early and my father ate by himself after work. The image of him sitting alone at the table is a memory that bothers me still.

For many families, solitary suppers are by-products of today's busy, overscheduled lives. Meals have become haphazard affairs, sandwiched between children's after-school activities and parents' evening meetings. Given the hassles of trying to coordinate four or five conflicting schedules, it's a wonder we get fed at all. Indeed, during the eighties, proper meals virtually vanished for many, replaced by snacks that were eaten on the run. Rather than "dine," people "grazed" like cattle, a habit that was bad for digestion and even worse for family life.

But as the nineties draw to a close and a new millennium begins, we seem to be coming back to our senses, with more of us recognizing the importance of combining nurturing with nutrition. Across the land, Americans are coming back to the table, in a nightly celebration of family life. We're coming back for a taste of the old-fashioned values that hold families together through difficult times; for the comfort of sharing life's ups and downs with our loved ones; for the chance to honor the mealtime traditions that brighten our days and form the basis for memories that will last forever. We're coming back because in a world that is moving too fast, families tend to drift apart, and because there's no better vehicle than the table for bringing them back together.

I have made it my mission to help families come back to the table to create their own traditions, small rituals and customs that convey the strong sense of shared identity that enables some families to withstand pressures that tear others apart. As you'll read in the following chapters, such traditions can be as simple as the apple turnover Carole Pagliarulo always found on her breakfast plate on her birthday, or as sweet as the banana splits Marcy Gold made for her children after their last day of school. They can be as basic as pancake breakfasts after church every Sunday, or family pizza parties on Fridays to celebrate the week's end. In short, anything that motivates you to spend quality time together—not the kind spent in front of the TV every night, or in the minivan en route to field hockey, but the kind where we all come together, face-to-face and eye-to-eye.

Somewhere, somehow, there's a little free time lurking in everyone's day. It just takes a bit of imagination to find it. For some families, breakfast may be the answer; for others, perhaps Sunday brunch. And there's no law against marshaling the troops to a restaurant, or serving Chinese takeout every now and again. Supermarket salad bars offer home cooks a jump start, as do ready-made pizza dough and sauce. The point is that somewhere between all and nothing, there lies a vast middle ground. And ultimately, *what* we eat matters less than the fact that we eat it together.

You'd think a woman whose mission and business revolve around cooking and creating traditions that stem from the table would have gotten an earlier start, but I didn't even begin learning to cook until my junior year of high school. And I might never have learned at all had it not been for two things: a failed typing test and a Ritz Cracker Mock Apple Pie.

I'd always been a good student, hardworking and determined. But the fact remains that I was awful at typing. My fingers were clumsy and I hit all the wrong keys. No matter how often I practiced, I was still the worst student in the class.

Thus, after six weeks of typing class I transferred to home economics, a course I'd always wanted to take. Oddly enough, it was that mock apple pie that hooked me. Transforming Ritz crackers and a few simple ingredients into something that passed for real apples seemed like pure magic in those days—right up there with spinning straw into gold. Intrigued, I knew I had found my true calling. From that day forward, I never looked back.

Home economics and I were made for each other. In the kitchen, I could create something beautiful and delicious that others could appreciate and share. I brought my enthusiasm home to my mother, and practical as she was, she indulged my culinary flights of fancy and delighted in the results. I remember clipping a recipe from the *Chicago Tribune* that called for eight flavors of sherbet for an ice cream bombe in the shape of an Easter egg. With my mother's blessing—and a large chunk of her grocery allowance—it adorned our table every Easter for years.

As a home economics major at the University of Illinois at Urbana, I expanded my culinary horizons, eagerly sharing my discoveries with my mother during my frequent visits back home. I wasn't just visiting Mother, however. I also came home to see Jay, my boyfriend since high school. Jay and I eventually married and set up housekeeping. Of course, I didn't always have as much time for cooking as I would have liked, but my new husband and I enjoyed sharing the details of our days over dinner at the table—it was where we'd catch up on the day's events.

As much as I loved teaching home economics, like many new mothers I jumped at the chance to stay home when my first daughter, Julie, was born. Those years at home gave me time to really indulge my love of cooking. I pored over cookbooks and invited friends and family over for dinner. I turned every holiday, even the lesser ones, into excuses for special theme dinners with family.

But all that came to an end when I started my business, The Pampered Chef, in 1980. Once again, I had limited time to fix family meals. But I knew how important the tradition of family dinners was, so I began to follow my mother's example, browning five pounds of meat at a time and trying to stay a few days ahead of the game by chopping extra onion or green pepper and wrapping it up to use later. I cooked on weekends and froze things; I simplified and I planned.

But over the years, I became busier and busier with my business. At first, my goals were modest, but my company took on a life of its own. I'd set out to help families share more mealtimes by making cooking faster and easier—and it was working. However, it was limiting the time I had to spend with my own family.

That first year, I was overwhelmed, not to mention excited, by the newness of it all. I'm afraid there were times when I grew quite obsessed with my new role as a fledgling entrepreneur, letting it consume too much family time. I'll never forget the night Julie and Kelley, my younger daughter, chided Jay and me for talking about nothing but business during dinner. They were right and we knew it. We apologized on the spot, promising to behave like parents as opposed to two people sharing a business dinner.

From time to time, I still needed reminding, however. Wearing multiple hats on one head gets confusing, as we all know. Today's parents aren't just parents. They're also tutors, coaches, referees, nutritionists, psychologists, babysitters, and pediatricians, to say nothing of their "day" jobs. The sheer number of roles we all play makes it difficult to keep life in perspective, to change hats as quickly and often as we should. Luckily, our children tend to be very good at reminding us that of all our jobs, that of parent is by far the most important.

After our scolding, Jay and I vowed to reform. From then on, work was largely off-limits over dinner. We had family discussions instead, about anything and everything our daughters brought up, and we often remained at the table long after we'd finished our meal.

All of that seems very long ago. These days, most of our family dinners take place on joyous occasions, like holidays, homecomings, and reunions. What was once an everyday occurrence, the four of us sitting down to dinner as a family, happens only now and then, making it that much more special. And these days, when I gather my family at the table, be it in person or in my mind's eye, a feeling of well-being envelops me. It's a feeling that lingers beyond the dinner hour and the cleanup, one I'll dip into again and again.

Feelings linger, but, alas, daughters do not. The years

pass so quickly, and our time with our children is so fleeting. One minute they're playing house with their baby dolls, and the next thing you know they have homes and lives of their own. We all complain about spending too much time at the office, but who among us regrets having spent too much time with our children? While I look back with fondness on my daughters' milestones, from their first steps all the way to their first dates, it's the everyday moments I cherish most: chopping vegetables in the kitchen while the girls sat at the table doing homework, sharing hot pancakes with them on a cold Sunday morning, or meatloaf on the odd Thursday night.

Ours is a close, tight-knit family; all those shared dinners have made our bonds strong. There will always be holidays, birthdays, and visits, but an era is ending. We'll no longer be sharing a home and a table, night after night, year after year. That, too, is as it should be, of course. Just as my sisters and I left our parents' table, so must my daughters leave mine. I'm not saying the next phase of life won't be happy. I'm just saying it won't be the same.

When I fast-forward the projector a few years into the future, I see lots of wonderful times ahead. I see my grandchildren joining us at the table in their high chairs, their first finger foods clutched in their chubby fists. But right now, I can't help but wish for a brief intermission, a short pause to reflect and regroup. Perhaps that's why I've summoned everyone back to the table, in my memories and on these pages. Maybe I just need one last look at the four of us just as we were: my little family, sharing our days and our dreams in a ritual timeless as love.

I also find myself wanting to share the bounty of a lifetime of family meals, those lessons we learned over tacos, the feelings that warmed us like stew, the problems that ceased to be problems after we'd passed them around with the rolls.

Along with my own memories, tips, and advice, in Come to the Table I'll serve up the best strategies I've gleaned from others for incorporating shared meals and celebrations into family life, the best ideas for bringing loved ones to the table. There'll be something for all types of families, be they blood or blended, colleagues or classmates, neighbors or friends. The importance of this daily ritual will be brought to light, and I hope to inspire you to bring your family back to the table.

So I invite you to make yourself comfortable, to turn off the TV and turn on the answering machine. Pour some tea, grab a sugar cookie, and join me on a journey through the dining room and into the heart.

Come to my table, where we will celebrate food and families, laughter and love.

Doris Christopher
November 1999

Celebrations

Like most people my age, I have a hard time remembering what it was like to be six. I have an equally tough time recalling how it felt to be four, or eleven, for that matter. But ask me what it was like to *turn* six, and it's a whole other story. On the topic of my sixth birthday, I can go on at great length.

I can tell you, for example, that on June 2, 1951, at my request, I had calf liver for dinner. And, much to their dismay, so did my two older sisters, having failed to talk me into asking my mother to make something—*anything*—else. Since I wouldn't eat a piece of liver today to save my life, I suspect I chose it precisely because my big sisters opposed it so violently. When you're the baby of the family, moments of power are rare. They're also addictive: I requested the same exact menu for the next three birthdays in a row.

We still laugh about my "liver years," my sisters and I, but in retrospect I think those dinners speak volumes about what it was like growing up as the junior member of the Ted Kelley family in Oak Lawn, Illinois, during the postwar years.

Birthday memories are like that. They're shorthand, in a way, for a bit of our personal history, a blast from our own distant past. A faded snapshot is all that's required to send us hurtling back through the decades. To this day, I can look at a picture of my family taken long ago and re-create my place in the universe as a child. It may have been at the bottom of the pecking order, but it was a wonderful place just the same. It was there that I learned all I needed to know about security, love, and belonging. It was there that I learned who I was.

The universe of my childhood no longer exists. But bits and pieces of that lost world remain with me: the meat grinder I inherited from my mother; my Aunt Anna's recipe for baked beans; the sense of well-being that still warms my heart at the sight of my family gathered around the table.

And when I close my eyes and let my mind wander into the past, I can picture us still, drifting one at a time on a cold winter evening into my mother's kitchen, five separate souls merging into one family, in a timeless celebration of what it means to belong. Back in my "liver years," of course, family meals weren't endangered. They were simply what families did. Whatever else our lives brought, here was something to count on, something to anchor the day. These celebrations of kinship and closeness always started with blessings and ended with sweets. Casual interruptions like phone calls weren't acceptable, either, although the phone seldom rang. When it did, my family would be startled, bewildered. Now who could *that* be, at *this* hour? It was suppertime, after all.

For the most part, the suppers of my growing-up years were fairly routine. We took our seats at the table between five and five-thirty and shared the events of the day over practical, easy meals that were hearty and economical, if a bit unexotic. Mind you, nobody ever complained; our daily bread was satisfying and tasty. But on birthdays and other special occasions, we would take a welcome break from our routine. On those evenings, "supper" became "dinner," a fancier-than-usual meal made all the more festive by the addition of a guest or two, along with a tablecloth and maybe even some hors d'oeuvres beforehand. The mere act of eating these tidbits in the living room, a place where food and drink normally were forbidden, heightened our anticipation, setting the tone for the dinner to follow. Our conversation was more animated and our laughter more frequent. We ate later than usual and we lingered a bit longer. Tomorrow, we all knew, we'd be eating Swiss steak off our everyday Melmac. But now, over roast beef and pie, we were happy to bask in the glow.

Those were among the memories I grew up with, of good times I hoped to re-create with my own children, who were born during the seventies, when shared mealtimes were still a fixture of American life. But during the eighties, as women, including myself, entered the workforce in record numbers and children's schedules became busier, things began to change. As a result, the family dinner hour seemed to be going the way of unlocked doors and bacon-and-egg breakfasts.

Nowadays, getting everyone to the table at the same time is easier said than done, especially when one child's soccer practice follows another's violin lesson, to say nothing of the nightly challenge of feeding a family made up of one vegetarian, one dieter, and a carnivorous teenager or two. And how do we cope when our schedules are at odds with our appetites—when the kids want to eat at five-thirty, but Dad won't be home until eight? What about the nights we're delayed at the office, and our good intentions all go up in smoke?

It is possible to reconcile today's hectic pace with our need to celebrate and connect with our families. What most of us need is a starting point, some means of taking that first, wobbly step toward the fridge and that vaguely familiar appliance, the stove. Let go of unrealistic expectations and impossible standards, and the side dish of guilt that goes with them. Times *have* changed; things *are* different. About the only things that haven't changed are our need to celebrate and to spend time with our families. And while it may no longer be realistic to expect the whole clan to march into the kitchen at five-thirty sharp every night, that isn't to say we can't get it together three nights a week, or even one. Don't view this tradition as a chore, but rather a celebration.

You can make the times you do come to the table as a family memorable. A few festive touches added to your family's meals can go a long way toward boosting everybody's enthusiasm. Along with improving your odds of getting things off to a good start, you'll also create some new ways to celebrate in the process. After all, when you stop and think about it, most families have a great deal to celebrate—not only birthdays, but weddings and anniversaries, new babies and new jobs, good report cards and graduations, promotions and winning sports teams. Celebrations are a great time to bring the family together. And, a good time to begin a few new family traditions.

When Sammy Werner's T-ball team won its championship, his mother, Claire, used simple food coloring to turn her family's supper into a tribute. The Werners ate orange mashed potatoes washed down with blue milk, in honor of Sammy's team colors. "Food coloring is fun, inexpensive, and easy," says Claire. "And it adds interest to foods kids won't otherwise eat. It amazed me how fast that blue milk disappeared!" These days, eight-year-old Sammy and his five-year-old sister, Ellie, never know what rainbow shades they might find on their plates. Claire added purple coloring to the vanilla cake mix for Ellie's Barney birthday cake. And green pancakes have become a weekend staple at the Werners' house.

As the Werners' story shows, kids love the little things that turn "ordinary" into "special." There are as many of these as there are families, and they needn't be costly or elaborate. The happy truth is, it takes surprisingly little to elevate a humdrum meal into a festive one. Chocolate milk in a wineglass. Ice cream sundaes for dessert. A special plate to mark special occasions. Celebratory traditions can be as easy as swapping seats, thereby giving the all-A student or Most Valuable Player a spot of honor at the head of the table. Families with round tables can accomplish much the same thing by serving their MVP first.

In the Christopher household years ago, celebration dinners were officially designated by the use of the colorful place cards my daughters made. We still use them for special occasions, even when it's only the four of us. My husband, Jay, has one decorated with a drawing of a necktie, and Kelley has one with a beer mug, a humorous nod to her college days. Julie, the shopper of the family, has an American Express card on hers. Mine has a house—our house—bright and welcoming, beneath a blue sky with white, puffy clouds. More than silver platters or crystal goblets, these little cards make us happy. They remind us that no one knows us better or loves us more than each other.

The special dinners I made for my daughters' birthdays further reflected their personalities. Over the years, I've cooked everything from chicken fajitas to shish kebab to satisfy the adventurous tastes of Kelley, my younger daughter. But for Julie, a hamburger lover, nothing but burgers would do. One year, in hopes of making memories along with dessert, I carried this theme all the way through to her birthday cake: a dead ringer for a giant Big Mac, with green-tinted icing for lettuce, chocolate icing for the burgers, peanut butter icing for the bun, and peanuts sprinkled on top just like sesame seeds!

Unusual birthday cakes have been a Christopher tradition ever since. The year Kelley turned five, I baked fancy individual cakes for a celebration that combined elements of dress-up with an old-fashioned tea party. Kelley and her guests sipped tea and ate their cakes while wearing their moms' Sunday best, complete with high heels and hats. On other birthdays, I remember pink-and-white checkerboard confections and Winnie the Pooh cakes, but every now and then, nostalgia triumphed over invention, and I opted instead for the rich chocolate layer cake with white icing my mother always made for my birthdays. I hoped my daughters' birthday memories would live on the way mine have, and that one day, they'd look back on their own "liver years."

As the familiar, rich scent of my children's cakes filled the air, transporting me back to my youth, I lingered awhile in the kitchen reliving those celebratory dining room dinners, mesmerized once again by their spell. Long after the birthday candles had been blown out and the wishes had come true (or not), our family memories of those dinners would continue to warm us, making us feel special and loved.

The fact that we'd had fun in the process made our bond that much stronger. And one of the main reasons my celebratory dinners loom so large in my memory is simply because they were fun. An underrated commodity in today's busy world, family fun often falls by the wayside, but its worth shouldn't be lost in mundane details of everyday life like household bills, disappointing report cards, and longer-than-usual work hours. Families that set aside time to have fun together are closer and happier as a result, a lesson brought home to me not just by my own parents, but also by my husband's, who believed it should be a priority all year long, but on birthdays in particular.

My in-laws, Maxine and Walter Christopher, always celebrated Walter's birthday by throwing a dinner party. Like the guest of honor, a sociable man who loved gag gifts and jokes, these parties were always great fun. The year Julie was born, we decided to turn Walter's annual party into a practical joke. The perfect vehicle for doing this was something we called a Mystery Dinner.

On the eve of Walter's birthday, the dinner guests were seated at a table set with nothing more than a centerpiece: no dishes, no flatware, no food. The puzzled guests were handed menus listing twenty items to be served in four courses. For each course, guests had to choose five items apiece. That may sound simple, but wait: every item, from flatware to apple pie, had been given a code name. To receive a spoon, for example, a guest had to order a "Fisherman's Friend," unlikely unless he or she happened to know that a "spoon" is also a type of fishing lure. "Barbells" were celery sticks with black olives stuck on either end. A "devil's tool" was a fork.

You can probably guess the result. Some guests got plenty of food but nothing to eat it with. Others got apple pie à la mode and a celery stick as their first course, followed by barbecued ribs and a spoon. It was a hilarious evening, filled with all manner of mismatches as Jay and I raced back and forth from the kitchen to the table, delivering one curious course after another. Small wonder I went into labor the next day! My in-laws insisted it was my hard work that night that brought Julie forth the next morning, on May twenty-first, Walter's birthday, and they're probably right. Either way, along with the family's first grandchild, a brand-new tradition was born. We've since given a number of Mystery Dinners for family members celebrating birthdays at both ends of the age spectrum, each as memorable as the first.

Nothing beats a birthday celebration, my family agrees, with the possible exception of *two* celebrations. In the case of the Graff family, it's more like a celebration and a half. "Chris and I started celebrating our children's 'half-birthdays' when they were little," Nancy Graff says, "but the ritual proved so popular, we've kept right on doing it, even though Garrett's now a junior in high school and Lindsay is in seventh grade." Her kids' half-birthdays, celebrated six months to the day after their actual birthdays, consist of special dinners of their choosing, and they differ from their true birthdays in several important ways. Instead of a whole cake, Nancy serves half a cake, with half the usual number of candles on top. There's just one present, costing no more than twenty dollars. And the guest list is limited to Garrett, Lindsay, Nancy, and Chris. "Real birthdays involve other people, but on half-birthdays, the focus is just on the family," explains Nancy. "And half-birthdays aren't really about presents. They're more about being *almost* ready to drive, or being *almost* a teenager."

Those of us who've celebrated dozens of birthdays tend to forget how significant turning a year older can be to a child—especially for the baby of the family. Each birthday brings some exciting new "privilege," from starting school to paying the "adult" price at the movies, and all deserve recognition at family celebrations. Indeed, some birthdays deserve extra-special treatment, since they imply a rite of passage that's particularly noteworthy. For Kelley's Sweet Sixteen, for example, we had a cake that resembled a driver's license. When Alison Caplain turned thirteen, her mother, Marcy, planned a special women-only celebration, followed by a hairstyling session and a department store makeover.

Regardless of age or motif, most younger kids' birthdays can be easily put together by one or two adults using standard components: other kids, a fun activity, ice cream and cake, along with presents, paper plates, and plenty of napkins. But as we get older, the formula changes as our focus shifts from presents to people. And for the people who love us, that can lead to a different sort of celebration— the kind that comes from the heart, as opposed to the shopping mall.

Lynn Jonas used to buy her grandmother, Sarah, jewelry

or clothes for her birthday. But now she buys groceries instead. The special birthday dinners she cooks for her grandmother every June are made all the more meaningful by the distance Lynn travels to make them—nearly two hundred miles each way, from her home in southern Connecticut to her grandmother's in central New Hampshire. The food is secondary to the ritual, which is all about spending time together. And for Lynn, there's no better place to celebrate than in her grandmother's old-fashioned kitchen. "Every item on the table brings back memories: the salt and pepper shakers, the sugar bowl, the coffee creamer. In fact, my grandmother still keeps them all on the same orange paint-by-numbers tray I made for her when I was seven!"

In my experience, that isn't unusual. Heirlooms are important to families, and they often play a significant role in celebrations. A great-aunt's hand-embroidered tablecloth or the Waterford candlesticks that passed through Ellis Island in Grandmother's steamer trunk speak to us of continuity and stability, heritage and love. But even the simplest objects—like my family's handmade paper place cards—can take on mythic proportions when they embody a sentiment that comes from the heart. I know of one family that uses an old patchwork quilt as a tablecloth on special occasions, to celebrate their Appalachian roots. Another covers their table with an ordinary white sheet

that turns into a giant birthday greeting card once it's been signed by their guests after dinner. Couples can adapt this tradition for anniversary celebrations by writing each other notes on the tablecloth year after year, thereby turning a sheet into a gigantic love letter, a record of their life together.

A special plate on the table—either a family treasure or a purchased "celebration plate"—is yet another method for transforming a routine dinner into a celebratory one, as Donna Linthicum found out a decade ago. It was a bright turquoise plate, with little yellow ducklings encircling a white rim, the sole survivor of Donna's three-piece set of baby dishes. The set had been a gift from her mother when Donna was three, the same age as her younger son, Adam. Over the years the plate had been forgotten, but when Donna's mother found it packed away in a closet, she returned it to Donna, who was quite unprepared for the sensation it caused. Both Adam and his six-year-old brother, Matthew, immediately confronted her, demanding to know who got to use the duck plate. "Nobody. It's for special times," Donna told them, putting the plate out of harm's way in her china cupboard, where it could be admired from a safe distance.

She thought that would be the end of it, but in fact, it was just the beginning. Whenever one of the boys did something noteworthy, his first question would be: Do I get the duck plate for this? Accordingly, the plate began making sporadic appearances on the Linthicums' table, and a little ceremony evolved to go with it. On duck plate nights, Donna summons her family to a table that's already set. "We see that someone has the duck plate tonight," she announces. No one may begin eating until after the recipient has described his accomplishment and accepted his praise. "It's so funny," Donna says. "The boys are thirteen and ten now, and whenever one of them accomplishes something, his first question is still, 'Is this duck plate–worthy?'" She's careful not to overdo it, lest the old plate lose its luster. But used judiciously, the ritual of the duck plate sends a powerful message to her kids: their parents are proud of them.

Like Matthew and Adam, most children derive a great sense of security from the rituals and traditions that accompany celebrations. Among the other, more obvious benefits, a tradition is a hedge against disappointment, for children and adults alike. When we know exactly what's coming, we can anticipate it with pleasure, free from the burden of our own expectations. In my family, anything done twice is considered tradition. More often than not, proposed changes are met with resistance, along with a chorus of that age-old refrain "But we *always* do it that way!"

And part of me understands these expectations perfectly, since I still trace my own sense of well-being to the rituals and anticipations of my youth. Even now, more than forty years later, I find it impossible to bring out the good china without thinking back to those special celebration dinners my mother made when I was a girl. Amy Chan wouldn't dream of celebrating the anniversary of her

American citizenship without the backyard barbecue she and her daughters have looked forward to every August for twenty-five years. Like the buttery shortbread the Phillipses bake during blizzards, or the French toast the Carrolls have for Saturday breakfasts, these kinds of traditions help define families. Each time we honor them, we celebrate who we are.

And each time we honor our children's accomplishments, we help set the stage for them to flourish as successful adults. Perhaps that's why some of the sweetest celebrations of all are the ones that recognize our kids' achievements, like the ice cream sundae parties Jay and I always had for our girls after their music recitals. There's something especially gratifying about rewards that were earned through hard work. No layer cake ever tastes quite as wonderful as the one that follows a triumphant school play. No corn ever quite measures up to that first ear eaten after the front teeth come in, or the braces come off. That first real dive (as opposed to a jump) off the high board . . . the first book report given before the whole class . . . the first grand slam home run in Babe Ruth League. All are deserving of a family's applause and approval. All are duck plate–worthy.

In conveying our pride and approval through these token gestures, we encourage a closeness of family. We also instill values in our children. These values may even find their way back to us in wonderfully unexpected ways, since affection breeds affection, and generous parents rear generous children. That lesson was brought home to Claire and Gerry Werner on their anniversary a few years ago. Their son, Sammy, was just five at the time, too young to stay home alone but old enough to recognize his mom's disappointment when the babysitter canceled at the last minute. Dinner was just about ready that night when Sammy appeared in the kitchen sporting a white towel over the arm of his Sunday school blazer. He got so caught up in his role as a self-styled waiter that he even wrote up a bill, payable in hugs and kisses and presented with a flourish at the end of the meal. As they settled the "check," it occurred to the Werners that the spirit in which they were raising their son was beginning to rub off on him.

They now make it a point to stay home on their anniversaries, as do Roger and Evelyn Gray, whose daughters, Chloe and Katie, are seven and twelve. "While we enjoy going out as a couple, this is one night we share with our girls," Evelyn says. For years, the Grays have celebrated their anniversary by re-creating their first married meal, from the Italian wedding soup appetizer to the green apple wedding cake they had for dessert. "We look at the pictures and listen to the music we played during our reception fifteen years ago. After dinner, the four of us dance together. We then go outside and pelt each other with rice.

Finally, we all go to sleep with what's left of the cake under our pillows." It's an evening of romance for all four Grays, and one they look forward to year after year.

Like birthdays and baseball playoffs, however, anniversaries come but once a year, whereas dinnertime rolls around nightly. And in the absence of special occasions, romance tends to make itself scarce when the average family sits down to dinner. Alas, cranky kids, tired parents, and overcooked broccoli do not a celebration make, and many a fantasy of the ideal family feast has given way to the reality of dinner-as-ordeal. We've all been there—and we'll undoubtedly go there again—because ultimately, there's nothing inherently magical about the table. It's up to us to transform it into our family's sacred place, where petty arguments and minor grievances are set aside in favor of higher pursuits: Appreciation. Spirituality. Joy. A place we visit in gratitude, not just for the food, but for the lives it sustains; where, for a few moments each day or even each week, we practice seeing past the little things that don't matter to the big things that do.

There is no better lesson to impart to our children than the simple act that gives meaning to life, for therein lies the purest form of celebration. It's up to each of us to decide how to teach this, but a table blessing is a good place to start. Expressing our gratitude for all that we have is a wonderful habit to get into, because the better we get at seeing the good things, the more we are able to see. And the better we get at transforming our tables into all that we want them to be.

In the process, we find, something magical happens. Life's background noises and daily distractions fade into the background. Over roast beef or spaghetti, we listen and learn, cope and compromise, remedy and resolve. And we celebrate, with blue milk and green pancakes, handmade place cards and cakes cut in half. We giggle and argue and pass the potatoes. We dance to life's music, and we come away humming the tune.

It is with that melody in my heart that I wish you a life-time of celebrations, happy birthdays and half-birthdays, too.

Sundays

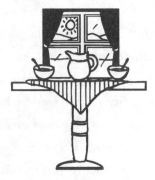

The best day of the week started with bacon and eggs and ended with Ed Sullivan. In between were fat newspapers and heavenly church choirs, droning lawn mowers and sweet ice cream cones. And right in the middle, the centerpiece of it all, was our family's Sunday dinner, a meal that did for our spirits what the morning sermon had done for our souls. Even now, more than forty years later, I still marvel at how seamlessly one ceremony flowed into the other; how natural it felt to walk home from church and take our seats at the family table. And so one week ended and another began, in an atmosphere of reflection and renewal.

We packed a lot into those long-ago Sundays: visits with relatives, ice cream outings, yard work, and trips to the roller rink. Is it just me, or did time seem to pass much more slowly on Sundays, as we sat around the table filling each other in on the events of the week, catching up on the tidbits of news families share with each other, and discussing our options for what we should do after the dishes were done? Somehow, those afternoons always stretched on and on to accommodate all of our plans.

Sundays had a quality all their own back in those days, a feeling quite unlike that of Tuesdays or Fridays or Saturdays. Sundays were spiritual. They stretched out before us, lazy and long, ideal for quiet reflection, relaxation, and togetherness, for putting our house in order, both literally and figuratively, before jumping back into the fray. There were no malls to rush off to, no shopping centers or giant "superstores." Folks went to church, then came back home to dinner. The sanctity of Sunday as "Family Day" was respected to a far greater degree.

Nowadays, for many people, Sunday is just another day in which to hunt for bargains, watch football on TV, or put in a few extra hours at the office to get a jump on the rest of the week. I know many couples who are forced to split up every Sunday, just to keep pace with their kids. Mothers drive daughters to swim meets or band practice; fathers take sons to hockey or Little League games. With most retail businesses staying open on Sundays, the competition for our families' time at the table is greater than ever before. And the notion of setting aside one day a week to spend with our families, to recharge our batteries, rest and reconnect, is in danger of becoming outmoded, a quaint relic of a simpler time.

And yet, never have we needed a day to replenish more than we need it right now, with today's frantic schedules and hectic lifestyles. Boundaries that were once so distinct—between home and office, workdays and weekends—have blurred, making it harder and harder to carve out time for ourselves.

Being overworked and overextended has even achieved a certain status, a certain cachet, in twentieth-century America, where it's become fashionable to be so busy that we barely have time to breathe. But I worry about a society that values productivity above all else: above time with our families, time for ourselves, time spent in service to others. Life is a balancing act, and when things get this off-balance, it takes a concerted effort to get back in sync. It takes Mom, Dad, and the kids around the table on Sunday, passing the pot roast and asking, "So, how was *your* week?"

I know only too well how easy it is to talk yourself out of this, to convince yourself you haven't the time. As Trish Klinger says, "There are Sundays when I think to myself, I have so much to do around the house that I really shouldn't go to Mom's today." And yet, she adds, "I always go. I remember how much fun it was to play with my cousins, and I need to talk to my sisters and catch up on the family news and gossip. . . . Sunday dinners at my mom's make me stop and take a break. My kids play with my sister's kids, and our husbands fall asleep on the recliners watching sports while my sisters and I talk and clean up. And throughout the week, as I catch up on the laundry and cleaning, I have funny moments and stories from Mom's kitchen table to remember and make me smile."

It needn't be some five-course extravaganza that brings families to the table on Sunday. Given the realities of modern life, and the demands on today's two-career couples, the era of big, fancy feasts is over, except on special occasions, of course. Susan Allshouse's mother, like many women of her generation, routinely spent her entire Sunday in the kitchen, whether she cared to or not. Sue speaks for a large share of *her* generation when she says, "I can honestly say that the old-fashioned Sunday dinner that I watched my mom go through does not interest me."

By contrast, Sue's children enjoy seeing their mom sit outside in a lawn chair watching them play basketball while she grills the steaks. "The main difference between then and now is that we are on the go much more and plan our meals around our events and our energy level," she says. "So a Sunday in the Allshouse household could be Domino's Pizza or a home-cooked meal. You never know.

But we do celebrate being together and find we connect so much better on the days we congregate around the dinner table."

The Swett family often eats out on Sundays, largely for the sake of convenience. But, as Cindi Swett says, "The nice thing is that all five of us are together, and when you think of it, I guess that's the important part. Just knowing you belong somewhere and are cared about is enough to make anyone's self-esteem climb the scale."

Indeed, looking back on my childhood Sundays, I now see just how precious they were. Those midday dinners my mother prepared gave me a sense of stability that has stayed with me throughout the years, defining family life and sowing the seeds for the relationships I now enjoy with my own daughters.

My mother's fried chicken wasn't the only reason those Sundays were special to me. More significant even than dinner was the fact that my father stayed home. Having him with us on Sunday—his only day off from his service station—changed our household dynamics in subtle yet wonderful ways. For one thing, my mother did no housework to speak of, except for the cooking, of course. My two older sisters—off doing their own thing all week—could be counted on to be there, too. And finally, we could go places on Sundays that we couldn't go during the week, since my mother never learned how to drive. As a result, our Sundays were rife with the promise of adventure and the contentment of having the people I loved most within sight. I wasn't just "me" anymore, not on Sunday. I was part of a family, one of "us."

And we made the most of our big day together, not just with bacon and eggs at breakfast, but with leisurely conversations over the dinner table during the one meal that never felt rushed. We discussed the events of the week—both in our lives and in the outside world. We ate slowly and went back for seconds, more to prolong the occasion than to quell any lingering hunger pangs.

The rest of the day may have been devoted to puttering, doing yard work, or reading the paper. Perhaps we'd all go for a ride in my dad's car, stopping at friends' or the ice cream parlor. Regardless of what we all ended up doing, we were more aware of each other's presence on Sundays, even when we were scattered throughout the house. Simply knowing we were all there together—under the very same roof—always made me feel extraordinarily safe. Often, when I talk with people who grew up with the tradition of Sunday dinner—people who can no longer recall what their families talked about or even what they ate—that feeling of safety is the recurring theme, the memory time can't erase.

Those slow, quiet Sundays we recall with such fondness may be a thing of the past, but we *can* recapture the wonderful closeness we experienced growing up, the feelings of safety and warmth, by reinstating the time-honored tradition of sharing Sunday dinner with our families. Not by baking our own bread, making pasta from scratch, or cooking a big meal, but by simply setting aside a portion of the day to share food, love, and laughter with our dear ones.

After all, it's the people who make the meal special; the food's nothing more than a prop. If you doubt it, consider the fact that while Arlene Wolf has wonderful memories of her mother's homemade ravioli—"the making of it, flour all over the place, wetting your fingers and folding the little triangles"—they are no more or less special than Pamela Gorman's recollections of *her* Sunday dinners, at a cafeteria buffet in Des Moines. Not cooking on Sunday is a time-honored tradition in Pamela's family. As her grandmother used to say, "Sunday is, after all, the Lord's day. He rested on the seventh day, and so will I."

"We would stand in that winding, Disneyland-style line for what seemed like hours," Pamela says. "With each turn, our anticipation would grow. What would we choose to eat this time?" It was always the same: ham, fries, and French silk pie for Pamela, roast beef, mashed potatoes, and cake for her sister, fried chicken, green beans, and custard cups for her grandparents. ("Take whatever you want," said her grandpa, "but you get a shampoo with whatever you don't finish," a threat that he never once carried out.) After dinner, the family would caravan back to Grandpa's house on a hill overlooking the airport, to spend the afternoon telling knock-knock jokes and watching the planes take off until the sun slipped down behind the trees.

Like the "arguments" Rachel Chobot always had with her grandfather over the best way to eat her grandmother's pie—fruit first versus crust first—and the tea towel fights Cindi Swett had with her brothers when they were supposed to be cleaning the kitchen, those cafeteria dinners were a sacred ritual.

But how do today's families create such venerable traditions, having grown accustomed to going our own separate ways? How do we convince our independent-minded offspring that Sunday dinner with the family beats a milkshake and fries at the mall? I think we begin by making attendance mandatory—after all, our parents never gave *us* a choice—and then softening the blow by making this meal truly special, one that everyone looks forward to, by creating an atmosphere that celebrates family life by encouraging every member's involvement.

Let your children take turns planning menus, choosing dinner music, or even coming up with topics to discuss. Alternate cooking at home with eating out, and let everyone take a turn choosing the restaurant. Once a month, invite someone special to join you: a teacher, a neighbor, a friend. Choose the guest or guests together, and let everyone help entertain them. Feast on favorite appetizers one week, create-your-own pizza the next. Invent a new holiday and make up your own rules for celebrating it, the sillier the better. Then put up notes informing your family that Go Backwards Day, say, will be observed in the dining room at six P.M. sharp, and that everyone is hereby expected to back into the room. You can then proceed to serve your family dessert first, one change of pace that is always a crowd-pleaser!

After a few suppers like these, your Sunday mealtime will start undergoing a transformation into an end-of-the-week celebration, a way of making the weekend last a bit longer. Not all at once but gradually, new rituals, which your family will come to look forward to, will start to take hold. In the meantime, a sense of humor—and realistic ex-pectations—are every bit as essential as serving food that your family enjoys.

That could mean homemade pizza, burgers and fries, or an occasional trip to a local fast-food place. It may even mean having breakfast instead, or everyone's favorite: Sun-day brunch. Pancakes, waffles, omelettes, and crepes all are easy enough to prepare, and a late-morning meal has the added advantage of leaving the afternoon free for a family bike ride, a trip to the movies, or a visit to a local amuse-ment park.

For Erin McNutt, who grew up with Sunday dinners of hamburgers, baked beans, and chips, tailoring menus to her health-conscious children, a daughter, sixteen, and son, twelve, is necessary for maintaining a solid dinner-table constituency. "In this family, the potato chips have been replaced by a great walk after the meal. This Califor-nia family is looking toward health, fitness, enjoyment, and the desire to create a haven, if only for a few short hours on a Sunday afternoon," Erin says.

Like many busy families, Erin's takes advantage of this set time together to make plans for the week ahead. Each Sunday along with their appetites, the McNutts bring their calendars to the table to discuss who'll need rides to and from after-school activities. These sessions give Erin a clear indication of her family's whereabouts, and bring about a smooth start to the week. They're also a good exercise in family problem solving, as the McNutts work together to head off potential conflicts *before* they arise.

For Debbie and Barry Braverman, whose son and daughter are thirteen and nine, Sunday nights used to be more frustrating than fun as Debbie struggled to get her children through their homework, baths, and shampoos after dinner. Eventually, it dawned on her that with nothing awaiting her kids besides bedtime, they had little incentive to hurry. The dawdling stopped as soon as she rearranged their routine so that homework and showers come first. "Now I tell them that if they're in their pajamas with their homework and baths done by dinnertime, we can all do something together afterward. We may clear away the dishes and bring out a board game, watch a movie, or read a good book. Our Sunday dinners are much more relaxing and enjoyable, and we get the week off to a much better start."

Like the McNutts, the Bravermans also linger at the table after their Sunday dinner, to clear the air at a family meeting. Ben might campaign for a later bedtime, while Zoe might lobby to watch more TV. Even if their requests are denied by their parents, "the kids feel better simply for having been heard," says their mother. Often, these mild gripe sessions inspire productive discussions about the reason for rules and routines. Invariably, they get everyone talking, which is, after all, the whole point.

It's also the point behind Sandy Hay's deck of topic cards. Each card deals with a subject the family thought would be fun to discuss. On slow conversation nights, one person picks a card from the deck and a family discussion ensues. Another approach is the game Evan and Claudia Moritz play with their children. "Best and Worst" was conceived as a way to encourage Samantha and Nicholas to express themselves and to fill their father in on all he'd missed while he was away on business during the week. Everyone takes turns listing the best and worst parts of their week. For Sam, that might entail having ice cream for dessert and falling down in the playground. For Nick, petting the neighbor's dog and having to go take a bath. Played weekly, Claudia says, "the game is a safe way for the kids to vent their unhappiness over some less-than-great moment, and to be reminded of something they enjoyed."

Bear in mind, some of the best family discussions occur spontaneously, just by virtue of sitting down together without any outside distractions, as Julie Strelow and her family discovered, quite by accident, recently. "We had gotten into the habit of plopping down in front of the TV, but something great happened: our TV in the living room suddenly died. Our family room is downstairs and not so convenient, so we have been sitting down at the dining room table as a family again," says Julie, who calls the broken

TV "one of the best things that has happened to our family."

Edna Abrams and her husband convene the whole gang—her children and her children's children—at her home on the first Sunday every month for the old-fashioned dinners Edna started cooking six years ago, after her son complained that he rarely got to see his sisters.

"These dinners are very special and nearly always have a theme. The actual food seems secondary, but the menus are put together thoughtfully to be very special, delicious, and beautiful to look at, and to incorporate everyone's favorite foods," Edna says. "Sometimes the children are able to help decorate for the dinner party. Balloons, streamers, flowers, drawings on the windows, or maybe cut-out paper snowflakes in the winter. We bring out the best china and stemware, even the dishes that have to be hand-washed. It often takes me two days after to put things away, but I love every minute of it. I'm sure these are some of the best days of our lives."

Families accustomed to eating their main meal after noon can extend that family feeling a bit longer by returning to the table in the evening to share a light supper or snack—a bonus for busy families that find it hard to get together during the week. Once my girls were older, I declared myself officially off-duty after making the big midday meal, leaving everyone else to fend for themselves in the evening. It's funny, but no sooner did one person get hungry and start rattling around in the kitchen than the rest of us would start straggling in. We might have ended up eating four entirely different suppers, but we invariably ate them together, continuing the conversation we'd had with our lunch.

Ken and Mary Bond have made their Sunday night suppers the one meal each week that they share with good friends. "Since we work very hard at eating together as a family every night and morning, we feel that Sunday is the day to share with others and enjoy good food and conversation." Similarly, Carol Olson and her family like to spend Sunday evenings with neighbors and friends, sharing a barbecue or a simple soup supper. "It gives us that family feeling even without always having our family close by," Carol says. If Sunday nights are a good time for you and your family to socialize, then by all means set an extra place or two at your table, and add some more vegetables to the stew.

Like her grandma before her, Pamela Gorman has a unique Sunday tradition for her family. They go out to Costco for pizza and fruit shakes, then plop their son into the carriage and cruise the aisles daydreaming about their future, a ritual that she calls "a little different, but really quite the same" as those cafeteria meals she shared with her grandparents.

Pamela last visited Des Moines for her grandmother's funeral, taking one last ride past the old house where she'd spent her childhood Sundays watching the airplanes take off. "I thought it would give me closure," she says, but instead, she found herself driving past a flat piece of land: both the house and the hill had been leveled. For a terrible moment, she thought nothing was left. Then she remembered all those cafeteria dinners—her grandparents' true legacy—and for the first time, she realized how important they were. "To this day, and even in this moment, my eyes get moist whenever I see one of those brown-and-white custard cups on a cafeteria buffet."

It's little rituals like these that hold families together,

that shape the memories we hold dear all our lives. If you still think you haven't the time for such things, please consider the following story a friend once shared with me, about a time-management expert who was brought into a company to address a group of busy executives. He began by placing a gallon-size wide-mouthed glass jar on a table and carefully filling it one at a time with a dozen or so fist-size rocks. When he couldn't fit any more rocks in the jar, he turned to his audience. "Is the jar full?" he asked. "Yes," they replied. The expert then lifted a bucket of gravel from under the table and began pouring it into the jar. As he shook the jar gently, small pieces of gravel worked their way into the spaces between the big rocks. "Now is it full?" he asked. But by this time, the executives were on to him. "Probably not," one said. "Good," said the expert, who reached for a pail and began pouring sand into the jar. As the fine grains of sand settled into the spaces between the rocks and the gravel, the speaker once again turned to the audience. "Now is the jar full?" he asked. "No!" the executives said. "Very good," said the expert, picking up a water pitcher and filling the jar up to the rim.

"Now, what do you suppose was the point of that exercise?" he asked. An eager executive raised his hand. "No matter how full your day is, you can always fit more in, provided you try hard enough," he said. "No, that's not it," said the expert.

"The point is that if you don't put the big rocks in first, you'll never get them in at all."

The next time you're struggling to squeeze in a meal with your family, take a deep breath and ask yourself: What are the "big rocks" in my life? Resolve not to let one more Sunday go by without remembering to put them in first.

Teenagers and the Table

Midway through the journey from childhood to adulthood lies the uncharted wilderness we call adolescence. It's a wondrous, mysterious place, a land of infinite possibilities, and no one who crosses it emerges unchanged. To parents whose offspring are just entering this territory, it resembles a primeval swamp filled with sinister forces that snatch sweet, compliant children and replace them with sullen strangers who look just like them, only taller. To those of us whose kids have already made the trip safely, it's more of a tropical paradise where the seedlings we tended so long and so carefully blossom before our very eyes.

But what we thought would be daisies sometimes pop up as thorny roses, taking us quite by surprise. Pot roast-loving daughters abruptly turn vegetarian. Aspiring quarterbacks put down their footballs and write terrible poetry instead. But that's the fun—and fascination—of teenagers, who alternately try on and discard new identities, often with dizzying speed. Our perceptions as parents are constantly challenged, along with our patience and our rules.

And while we can't wait til it's over, there *is* something thrilling about watching a person take shape, especially someone we diapered not that long ago. And therein, of course, lies the rub. For it's those dueling desires for the safe haven of childhood versus the exhilarating freedom of adulthood that are responsible for this new tension between us and our teens—that and our own tug-of-war between holding on and letting go.

Once, we could make every hurt go away with nothing more than a kiss and a hug. Soon, the child whose scraped knee we healed with a Band-Aid will have to learn to brush herself off and go on. Assuming we've done our job well, she'll be able to bounce right back up. But for these next few years, we'll have to watch as she stumbles. And we'll be the ones who will bleed.

So how do we survive our children's adolescence with our relationships—and our sanity—intact? We do it, in part, by recognizing this stage as a balancing act between youth and maturity, between familiar traditions and innovative new ones, between old rules and new flexibility. We do it by understanding our teenagers' contradictory needs for stability and freedom by providing a blend of the two. And finally, we do it by becoming a little more supple ourselves, and by learning to loosen up and "go with the flow."

That isn't to say we should start acting like teenagers. It *is* saying our lives and the lives of our children are changing in myriad ways as they struggle to become independent. The challenge for us is to respect that struggle and give them the space that they need. At the same time, we need to maintain the connection that will give them the confidence to grow. As every parent who's done it will tell you, that is a real tightrope act.

And yet it can be done—and done well—provided we maintain our humor, as Erin McNutt can attest. For it was her daughter, Amanda, who traded pot roast for vegetables soon after turning sixteen. Beef was the first to go, as of October. Three months later, Amanda quit pork, followed by turkey and chicken. Fortunately, Erin knew better than to take her daughter's new eating habits personally; instead, she resolved to face up to the challenge with her usual good nature intact. As Erin points out, "This is harder for me than her. Believe me, I cringe when I notice only rice and veggies going down her hatch. Of course, she is really active, eats the way the

Food Guide Pyramid suggests, and never gets sick. Fine! Be that way!"

Ultimately, Erin jumped on the bandwagon with her daughter, having gotten hooked on her own healthy food plan. Now, mother and daughter eat healthy food together, and Erin gives Amanda the credit for having challenged her to explore new ways of improving her own nutrition, an outcome that has further strengthened their bond. If you, too, have a vegetarian in the family, make a commitment to nonmeat meals at least once a week, and enlist your child's help in finding and preparing tasty nutritious new recipes. Vegetables that are frequently served as side dishes—baked potatoes, say—can instead assume a starring role in the meal with added toppings such as grated cheese, salsa, meatless chili, stir-fried vegetables, and sour cream. Or prepare a large salad filled with fresh, colorful vegetables and pass bowls of cooked shrimp or marinated beef or chicken strips for those who wish to add them. It's easy to accommodate dietary preferences; all it takes is a little bit of planning, and the results will go a long way toward showing your teenager you respect him or her as a person. And simply by making the effort, you will greatly reduce the chances of turning your evening meal into a battleground.

On the contrary, the table can be a powerful tool for families struggling to cope with adolescence, by providing the common ground on which parents and teenagers can meet, at least for a little while, every night. Jay and I discovered this firsthand when our younger daughter, Kelley, was in high school, struggling to cope with the difficult transition to adulthood.

Fortunately for us, by the time Kelley became a teenager, we already had a long-standing tradition of using our time at the dinner table for lively family discussions. When her older sister, Julie, passed through her teens, we talked about everything, from how to repair wounded friendships to how to handle rejection. Other topics ran the gamut: Why doesn't he call? What if I don't get invited? What if I don't like my date? These and other questions flowed out of Julie like water. We talked about manners and morals, values and careers. Peer pressure. College.

Throughout Julie's adolescence, we continued to be at the center of her life, along with her friends and her schoolwork, just as we'd always been, sharing her ups and downs and offering advice when it was needed. Her adolescence passed so smoothly that I must confess, there were times when Jay and I wondered what all the fuss was about! We found out two years later with Kelley, whose behavior was much more typical of the average angst-ridden teenager.

The flow of information Kelley once shared so readily

with us suddenly slowed to a trickle. She no longer wanted to do things with her family, and there were times when it seemed as if Kelley were making it her life's work to keep us from knowing anything about her schoolwork, her friends, or her life. She seemed increasingly guarded and unhappy, and we simply didn't know what to do. We could feel her slipping away from us and we were scared.

Over dinner, though, Kelley's hostility lessened. It was the only time we could communicate with her—at the table, where we'd talked over so many things in the past. Kelley had always liked my cooking, and over tacos or hamburgers, she'd slip back into her old pattern of opening up and sharing with us. For a little while, we'd have our little girl back. It was the one family ritual she seemed to respect, and I used it to our advantage, cooking up all her favorites—anything to draw her back to us. Telling stories and making references to funny things that happened during her childhood—or my own—helped to further restore our connection, and we lingered over those dinners as long as we could. What had occasionally seemed like a chore turned into a blessing, for which I was eternally grateful. Would we have weathered Kelley's adolescence without these family dinners? I'd like to think so. Still, the experience made me a believer in the value of shared mealtimes for families.

Fortunately, Kelley's difficulties turned out to be temporary and minor, although they certainly loomed large for us at the time, as these things tend to do both for parents and teenagers. But what feels like a crisis as it's happening often proves far less significant over time. Keeping that in mind may make it easier for you to focus on helping your child develop the self-esteem needed to weather typical adolescent storms.

If nothing else, adolescence is a humbling time for most parents, who need every conceivable advantage. In our experience, the most effective of these was the family table, and others I've talked with agree.

I cannot overstate the importance of establishing regular family mealtimes *before* children enter their teens. It is far more difficult to get older kids into the habit of sharing the dinner hour with their families than it is to simply continue the practice into their teen years. So my first piece of advice is to start early, when the idea of sitting down to dinner as a family is far more likely to generate a positive response. As Lisa Walker says, "I set the pace early on. My children have always gathered around the table—it's just the normal thing to do. It goes without questioning."

But you needn't despair if you happen to be a more recent convert. Better late than never, and there are ways of easing your adolescent offspring into this new routine with a minimum of grumbling on their part and a minimum of grief on your own.

First off, try assigning your teenager his or her own night to cook. Unlike doing the dishes—the chore most kids get stuck with, and their least favorite, from what I have seen—cooking dinner can be highly creative. It can also be billed as a preview of what the not-so-distant future will hold. Teenagers love being reminded that soon they will be on their own. From a practical standpoint, it makes sense for them to start learning the skills they'll need to take care of themselves. So go ahead: let them loose in the kitchen, and stay out unless they ask for help. Now's the time for them to develop their own tastes, and they can't do that if you're running the show.

Regardless of who's cooking dinner, try to let it be known that serious arguments have no place at your table. Mealtime should be pleasant, a means of providing not only nourishment but also a respite from the stress of the day. To that end, make it a point to focus on neutral topics, and while it's okay to solicit responses, try not to let family dinners deteriorate into the sort of interrogation sessions that invariably elicit sullen, one-word nonanswers. When you do ask your kids questions, try to make them specific.

As Amy Phillips has discovered, through countless conversations with Jesse, her fifteen-year-old, "a question like 'what did you do in school today?' is apt to generate a reply of 'nothing,' whereas 'what did they serve for lunch in the cafeteria?' is more likely to prompt some discussion." Amy also recommends asking your child's opinion and letting her know that you value it: So-and-so's son is getting bullied on his way home from school. What do you think he should do? Encourage constructive differences of opinion, as opposed to arguments and insults among siblings.

"Ask questions not just about test scores and term papers, but about things that truly matter to your kids, like the sports they play," suggests Alex Moran, whose two boys are seldom seen out of uniform. "And whenever possible, come to the table ready to share a laugh, whether it's a comic strip clipped from the newspaper or a joke someone told you at work." Alex's favorite source of humorous material these days is the Internet and the many friends with whom she exchanges e-mail.

Come to the Table

The bottom line: Strive for more fun and less criticism, and remember that giving orders with regard to haircuts, curfews, or choice of attire isn't the same as conversation. Endless bickering between siblings isn't either, and you may wish to declare it illegal. Make violations punishable by fines of up to a dollar, with the money put into a kitty for restaurant meals, take-out pizza, or other treats. Or, for each insult hurled, make the speaker come up with ten things he *loves* about his little sister. I guarantee everyone will be smiling again long before the list is complete.

New research has shown that while girls are more likely to speak in response to ongoing conversation, boys are more apt to stay silent when others are talking. So if you want to engage your son in conversation, ask a question and then stop talking to give him time to answer. And consider the possibility that a child of either sex may be more forthcoming when the two of you are alone.

If that seems to be true of your teenager, learn to seize those opportunities whenever—and wherever—they occur, be it in the car, on your bikes, or under the basketball hoop. After all, there is no rule book that says you must be seated at the table in order to talk with your kids.

Speaking of rules, don't hesitate to break them, at least on occasion. Sue Allshouse's kids know that whenever take-out pizza is on the menu, they're allowed to enjoy it in the family room in front of the TV—the lone exception to the house rule that all meals must be eaten at the table. "It is their treat and I think this is important," says Sue. "We are flexible, not rigid." Indeed, it never hurts to make an exception; you may even find your children more forthcoming as a result. Choose a night when everyone's favorite show is on, or when you've rented a video the whole gang wants to see. Just serve something relatively easy to eat; save the spaghetti with red sauce for some other night.

When Stacey Schrock's children reach their teen years, she will borrow a page from her own parents' book by allowing her kids' friends—male or female—to eat with them anytime, a policy Stacey calls "the greatest thing my parents did to keep me at the table" when she was a teenager. "It didn't matter if it was Sunday night dinner at Grandma's house or going out with my parents on Friday night," Stacey recalls. "The most important thing was that having a friend over for dinner didn't even count as one of my two 'date nights' allowed during the week. Looking back, I see a lot of benefits to this policy—they knew exactly where I was and who I was with!"

Patti Reid, who has survived her kids' teen years in style, agrees, adding that "friends are a great source of information, particularly if the friend and your teenager view themselves as (a) the final word on what's wrong with everyone else at school or (b) a comedy act. Mealtime performances can be hilarious, especially when they laugh so hard at their own shtick that milk comes out their noses."

On a slightly more serious note, Patti advises choosing a meal that involves some hands-on participation, such as make-your-own pizza or build-your-own tacos or fajitas, a tactic that works particularly well on boys. "If your teenager is a girl, however, you must be ready for the inevitable switch to vegetarianism. Now, the idea is to keep working until you find one dish she really likes that involves her favorite food items of the moment." In the case of her daughter, Amanda, now twenty, the recipe that resulted consisted of penne pasta with tomato sauce, goat cheese, and artichoke hearts, followed by a great dessert from the local catering shop (anything involving copious amounts of chocolate). Another successful ploy: calling in an order to Amanda's favorite deli, then asking her to go pick it up. This worked well for two reasons: it gave Amanda an excuse to drive the family car, and it enabled her to run into friends, out doing the same for *their* families.

Vegetarians and meat-eaters alike would no doubt enjoy the novelty of eating favorite breakfast foods for dinner. Cindi Swett tried it recently, and was amazed at her children's response. "You'd think we were having lobster tail," Cindi says. "The children were so excited they couldn't stop giggling. Even my teenager loved it." Cindi served cheese omelettes, orange Danish, and corned beef hash, a meal that will become a new monthly tradition. Other possible breakfast-for-dinner menus include bagels and smoked salmon, pancakes and sausage, or cereal with fresh fruit and muffins. Try make-your-own yogurt parfaits with assorted flavors of yogurt topped with granola, dried fruits, sweetened, pureed berries, and chopped nuts. Quiches, oatmeal, and savory bread puddings are other easy, nutritious, and fun dishes your family will be pleasantly surprised to see after dark.

Karen Hagen livens up her dinner table using a radically different method. "Our family is a noisy one, with three boys all vying for attention at the table," she says. "Sometimes, as I try to listen to multiple conversations all happening at once, all three boys complaining about rules or homework, shouting or interrupting, I have to remind my-self that mealtimes are to be treasured, not dreaded! But once in a while, someone suggests we have Joke Night and I'm sooo glad to be home."

For the record, the Hagens are not professional comedi-ans. "Some would even argue that we are pretty poor ama-teurs," Karen says. The family drags out the same old jokes every time: "Do you know what burns my tail? A flame about this high." Or "A horse walks into a store. The store-keeper says, 'Why the long face?'" Nonetheless, Karen says, "We laugh every time as everyone takes a turn. Once in a while, a new joke joins the fold. Once in a great while, even I can remember a joke long enough to retell it." The point is, every Joke Night ends with the Hagens all leaving the table smiling. The youngest, TJ, feels more confident, having had his say among his older brothers. Trevor, the middle son, feels he's come that much closer to perfecting his comic timing. And Kyle, the teenager, is reminded that his parents are still fun to be around. "My husband, Sean, and I get to hear from the boys in a very relaxed and hon-est way—no interrogations necessary." The bottom line: "I have no idea how Joke Night started," says Karen, "but I hope it's a tradition that will be continued long into my family's future."

I hope so, too, because studies show that teenagers who eat with their families are less apt to get into trouble and more likely to do well in school. Of course, none of us can hope to accomplish all this without *getting* our kids to participate in the evening meal in the first place. This may require a few drastic measures, at least in the very beginning. Take the Gibsons, for example. When Kelly, the oldest of five, was in junior high school, her parents initiated an unusual ritual in order to get everyone involved. "I usually didn't have any reservations relating the events of the day at the dinner table, but two of my brothers were especially quiet. They never really entered into the family conversation unless they were asked direct questions. Mom and Dad always wanted to 'stay in touch' with us, so when they had a particularly difficult time getting Kent or Kit to open up, one of them would say something like, 'Okay, it's time for everyone to take their turn.'

"This was usually met with groans of dread. Dad would start and give us his heartiest laugh, then it was Mom's turn. She would do something really off-the-wall, like an operatic 'hee hee hee hee' up and down the musical scale. By the time we got around the table (each of us forced to take our turn with a laugh) we were all in fits of hysterics. In spite of our protests, the tradition facilitated great conversations. Imagine my future husband's surprise and wonder at such an event several months after his introduction to our family. Now he's the one who pulls it on our kids when they are grumpy or nontalkative."

Come to the Table

When Robin Stretch-Crocker was growing up, her father took a different approach that proved every bit as effective. "My sister and I would play outside all day and when my parents would call us in for dinner, we would go inside reluctantly, eat our dinner as fast as we could, and then run outside to keep playing," Robin says. "One night, my dad had had enough of our eat-and-run attitude, and he made a new household rule: we had to sit at the table for at least thirty minutes, whether we were done eating or not. Boy, were we mad! For the first two or three days, we fought the new rule, but Dad stuck to his guns, and by the end of the week, something amazing happened: First, we were eating our dinner slowly enough to taste it. And second, we were staying at the table longer than the required thirty minutes! We were enjoying each other's company and talking as a family. Often, we would sit at the table for an hour or two without even wanting to go back outside."

As Robin grew older, she came to treasure these dinners with her family, which were often the only time they had to be together. "To this day, I am still very close to my parents, and I cherish our time together. If Dad hadn't stepped in and made his thirty-minute rule, our relationship might be different today, twenty years later."

As Robin's example shows, we mustn't be afraid to make rules for our children—not even those "children" who will soon be adults. So go ahead: Ban nonemergency phone calls during dinner. Institute a Thirty-Minute Rule. Forbid fruitless bickering or stressful topics during mealtime. Encourage your teenagers to tell jokes, invite friends, or laugh their way up and down the scale. Cook and eat vegetarian meals with your daughters, *without* any disparaging remarks. Plan some build-your-own menus for sons. And don't be afraid to let teenagers off the hook every now and then, on nights when they least expect it. Give them permission to watch TV and eat pizza, or go to the mall with their friends.

Little by little, they'll start opening up—not because they're being forced to, but because they're becoming comfortable enough to want to. Not every night, certainly, but at least now and then. "Please don't think it was a joyful dinner every night," says Rochelle Hoffman, whose kids are now twenty-seven and thirty. "There were many arguments and 'discussions' about being out of touch and not understanding, or about being the only one at school who can't . . . but through it all, dinner was the only time we were all together, for better or for worse."

Remember, chances to connect with our kids don't always occur between the hours of five and seven, so learn to recognize opportunities as they arise. Wait up for your kids when they go out at night—not to yell at them for coming in a few minutes past curfew, but simply to share some hot cocoa and a snack. Sit at the table together, just the two of you. Relax and let the conversation flow. Resist the urge to be judgmental; instead, treat your child like the young adult he or she will soon be. Treasure these moments alone with your child. From here on in, they will be rare.

Winter Comforts

When the days begin to grow shorter and the first au-
tumn leaves flutter down from the trees, I find it
helps to remember that the season of ice and snow is also
the season of savory meatloaf and garlic mashed potatoes;
that the same months that give us chapped lips and numb
fingers also bring crackling fires and soft flannel sheets. For
every hardship that winter affords, I believe it's possible to
find something cozy and warm to offset it. But to truly appreciate the comforts of the season, we must weather its
hardships as well, for it is only after having been *out* in the
elements that we can fully appreciate being *in*.

Of course, being out has its own joys to offer, like the
hush that falls over the landscape along with a thick, fluffy
frosting of snow, or the dazzling sparkle of sunlight on ice

that puts even Tiffany's windows to shame. Needless to say, such pleasures are not for the faint of heart or the weak of spirit. Just ask any child who's ever struggled into boots, parka, hat, mittens, and scarf for the privilege of making those first footprints in the freshly fallen snow: the key to enjoying the wonders of winter lies in carefully planning ahead.

The same holds true for winter's other, less obvious benefits, like the feeling of deep satisfaction that comes over us as we survey our packed freezers, full pantries, and neatly stacked cords of wood. The rituals of preparation themselves make us happy, and that can be most therapeutic. As winter arrives, we begin to set aside the more trivial aspects of human existence in order to better focus on life's fundamentals.

For most of us, those "fundamentals" are our loved ones, whose safety and well-being are of paramount importance to us. This isn't any less true during the rest of the year, of course, but I find myself dwelling on it even more during the cold-weather months, when I compulsively remind everyone to keep warm and drive safely, as I hug them a little more tightly at the door. Slick roads and flu epidemics are by no means the only dangers we face in life, but they do serve to remind us not to take anything for granted—least of all the people we love. And the cold weather inspires us to cuddle up with the ones we love. After all, what better winter activity is there than spending time indoors with your family, creating rituals that help keep everyone feeling warm, cozy, and loved?

We often enfold our loved ones in a metaphoric "embrace" of homemade soups and steaming hot chocolate, warm gingerbread and pots of brewed tea, much as our mothers once did for us. I still remember walking in the door to the aroma of my mother's vegetable beef soup, the best possible smell to come home to on a frigid Illinois afternoon. Once inside, I invariably made a beeline for the hot-air register in the hallway, assuming I was able to get to it first. There, I would sift through the mail we kept stacked on a table, as the feeling slowly crept back into my fingers and toes. That heat register was such a popular destination in our household in winter that there was even a mark on the wall from all our years of leaning up against it!

Then, as now, the greatest reward for any winter outing was the moment of coming back in. If you're anything like me, you probably head straight for the kitchen, since that tends to be the warmest room of all. My mother always seemed to spend more time in the kitchen during the winter, and I have to admit, I do, too. Cold weekends are perfect for cooking and baking; with the furnace running, homemade bread rises more quickly, and the idea of tending the soup pot or watching over the stew is sud-

denly very appealing. Soup, chili, pot roast, and other
hearty one-dish meals that go together with ease but that
require hours of simmering are the home cook's best
friend during the winter.

Wonderful smells fill the house as the soup, stew, or chili
bubbles away—hours of free advertising for the cook that
practically guarantees perfect attendance at the dinner table,
to say nothing of hearty appetites. And there's something
downright delicious about having everyone home when the
wind howls and the mercury drops; a sense of well-being that
is unsurpassed by anything else that I know. Add a fire in the
fireplace and a gathering storm, and there you have it: a
recipe for the ideal way to spend a frigid midwinter afternoon.

In order to brighten up the kitchen for these cozy
meals—which are often eaten without much sunlight,
given the limited supply of sun we get during the winter
months—buy a few pots of fresh herbs to place on the
windowsill, or a bouquet of fresh flowers to use as a centerpiece. If it's not there already, try moving your kitchen
table to the room's sunniest corner and surrounding it
with beautiful potted plants, either on a deep windowsill
or on plant stands. Hang a bird feeder outside your
kitchen window, or stuff giant pinecones with a mixture
of creamy peanut butter, raisins, and birdseed and hang
them on the branches of a nearby tree, making sure to

place the treats a safe distance away so the birds aren't in danger of flying into a window. You'll be rewarded with hours of colorful entertainment that will brighten up the meals you have on even the bleakest winter days.

Along with the music of the birds, try enhancing your cooking or eating atmosphere by listening to soothing classical, harmonious folk, or energizing rock music. Music in the kitchen can help you get a rhythm going that can greatly reduce the drudgery of highly repetitive chores such as floor scrubbing, oven cleaning, or dishwashing.

As long as you're already cooking, why not make several suppers at once? It doesn't take a lot longer to chop an extra onion or two, or to brown another pound of ground beef. For the same simmering time, you could have the week's cooking behind you, and best of all, you'll only have to scour your pots and pans once. Not to mention the fact that the majority of soups, stews, spaghetti sauces, and roasts seem to taste even better a day or two after they're made, once their flavors have had a chance to deepen and blend.

Given the Midwest's unpredictable weather and the demands of my own full-time job, I find having a few extra meals stashed away in my freezer as valuable as money in the bank. No wonder we refer to it as investment cooking! You never know when your investment will pay off, as it did for Toni Strazza and her family, when they were forced to weather a week-long blizzard on New York's Long Island years ago. With their electricity knocked out for seven long days and nights, Toni, her brother and sister, and their parents camped out in the den, warmed by a fire in the fireplace that did the work of their lights, furnace, oven, and hot-water heater. "Mom and Dad cooked using the fireplace and Grandma's cast iron cookware," Toni says. "With the electricity out, we had to eat everything in the house so the food wouldn't spoil." The investment meals came in handy. But, the Strazzas also had to improvise. "Dad taught us how to cook. He made red gravy, then poached eggs in it, topped them with mozzarella cheese, and served them over Italian bread in a bowl. He made the best chicken stew we'd ever had."

Normally, Toni's father traveled all week, and the kids only saw him on weekends, which made the Strazza family's Blizzard Week even more memorable. "We played cards and games all day and night," Toni recalls. "My sister and I had a dance contest to the radio. We melted chocolate bars and made hot chocolate with dry milk and water." And what could easily have been an ordeal instead turned into a festive week-long party, one the Strazzas will never forget. "If I were able to ask my family what was the single most favorite time in their lives, I can almost guarantee they would talk about this week," Toni says.

Here's hoping *your* lights don't go out this winter, but if they do, remember Toni's story, and treat the experience as a family adventure—although preferably a much shorter one!

Of course, you needn't wait for the lights to go out to enjoy a "camp out" at home with your children. It's easy enough to roast wieners and marshmallows over a wood fire, and even if you don't care to cook in your fireplace, you can always serve a cozy dinner in front of it, the way my mother-in-law, Maxine, used to do when Jay and his brother were little.

If you don't have a fireplace, your family can still enjoy a change of scenery along with their dinner. Spread a blanket on the floor of the living room or den for a midwinter picnic, the way Sandy Hay and her family do, or pull couch cushions up to the coffee table. Turn off the lamps and dine by candlelight—or by the light of the flame under your fondue pot. Dipping bread into hot cheese or fruit into warm chocolate sauce is a wonderful wintertime ritual that's been making a stylish comeback in recent years, so now's the time to dust off that fondue set you've kept stashed in the basement for so long. For an extra warm, fuzzy feeling during your family's Fondue Night, invite everyone to attend in their pajamas, bathrobes, and slippers!

The urge to hibernate tends to come over us all with a power and intensity that cuts across species, sending us crawling back into bed or burrowing into the sofa at the first whiff of snow in the air. Unlike bears, we humans approach our winter slumbers armed with knitting, needlepoint, newspapers, magazines, and books, to say nothing of cinnamon toast, grilled cheese sandwiches, and homemade Snickerdoodles fresh from the oven. There are few experiences in life as luxurious as that first winter's nap on a raw Sunday in January, when the house is warm and quiet and the sky is an ominous gun-metal gray. I'm a firm believer in the revitalizing powers of the occasional afternoon snooze, but there are lesser degrees of "cocooning" that accomplish much the same thing without so much as a smidgen of guilt, and there's nothing to stop the entire family from joining in.

Start in the den or family room, with some soft, soothing music and an assortment of blankets and quilts. Have everyone bring a book, or read one out loud together, perhaps a story set in frontier times detailing the considerable hardships of a family's first pioneer winter. A film festival starring your favorite movie videos is a good alternative, served up with plenty of hot buttered popcorn. Or dig out the Scrabble or Trivial Pursuit games and have your own family tournament. A challenging jigsaw puzzle—the more pieces, the better—is yet another activity everyone can enjoy.

The craving to hunker down is such a compelling one that people who live in more temperate climates often go to great lengths to simulate wintry conditions. At the first sign of a cool breeze, Jeannie Chabolla makes homemade chicken soup for her California kids, even if they're still playing outside in their shirtsleeves. Shannon Werhanowicz, another Californian, breaks out the hot chocolate and waffles the minute the temperature drops. And when rain falls on a Saturday, she and her husband hole up in the living room with their daughters, enjoying old movies and popcorn. "To fight off the 'blahs,' Dad helps them build a huge fort, with blankets draped over and around furniture and passageways to crawl through," Shannon says. "And I listen to classical music as I clean the house, with homemade soup simmering on the stove."

During the winter months, the kitchen can assume the role of "den" for the modern hibernating family, as it does for the Ameses when rain keeps their children indoors. Kathy Ames, a seventh-generation Californian, turns her table into an activity center where her kids bake cookies, work on photo albums, and play "office." Lisa Walker and her family like to play cards and dice games around their table, and with children ranging in age from five to seventeen, "We often have to form teams to play games that aren't usually played that way, so that we can all join together," Lisa says. "Not only do we laugh a lot, but it's great to see the big ones helping the little ones learn numbers. This isn't just good family time, it's a great teaching and learning experience that they don't even realize because of the fun." To brush up on multiplication tables, Janette Goerdt recommends rediscovering dominoes, which "absolutely must be played with at the table," according to Janette, who started playing with friends last year.

Writing letters is another painless learning exercise and a great winter pastime that can easily be expanded into a family activity. Rather than have each child write his or her own letter, a prospect that can be a bit daunting, have everyone contribute a few lines to the same letter, each using a different shade of ink. Only the signatures at the bottom, each one written in the author's assigned color, reveal which family member wrote what. Or, for a true Mystery Letter, leave off the signatures and make the recipient guess. What grandparent wouldn't be thrilled to solve such a tantalizing mystery!

Like the Ameses and the Walkers, the Madson kids' search for something entertaining to do in bad weather always seems to lead back to the table. "Hours are spent drawing pictures with pencil, crayon, marker, paint, and stickers as I work at the counter on business or on food preparation," Joyce Madson says.

All manner of crafts can be made at the table, from bread-dough sculptures or ornaments to polymer beads for hand-strung necklaces. I know of a number of families who use their tables as a work space on which to decorate cookies, paint by numbers, or build model airplanes or cars. The Nelsestuen family likes to come to the table to pore over mail-order catalogs. Few children would decline an invitation to spend a snowy day drafting their annual "wish list"

for Santa, and few grownups would turn down an opportunity to get a jump on their holiday shopping without the hassles of a trip to the mall.

These and other snuggly, indoor activities—making homemade pizza, folding clean clothes still warm from the dryer, coloring, composing a family newsletter—can carry you and yours through weeks of terrible weather in soothing and congenial style. But sooner or later, assuming your winters last as long as ours do, cabin fever will undoubtedly set in. And when it does, it pays to remember that some of the best winter adventures of all take place out-of-doors, often right in our own snowy neighborhoods. They're made all the more memorable and enjoyable when everyone in the family joins in, so don't be afraid to bundle up and get out there! Build a snowman, make some snow "angels," rent skates, strap on cross-country skis, feed the birds, ride a sled, build a fort, or just take a walk.

Still, no matter how much your family enjoys the season, after all is said and done, there *does* come a point—usually toward the end of February—when the novelty starts to wear off. Snowstorms that were grounds for celebration earlier in the season—particularly the ones that resulted in an unexpected holiday from school—suddenly elicit a chorus of groans, to say nothing of the children's response! For those of us who live in areas where winter tends to outlast its welcome, now is the season of our discontent, when too many snowstorms and too much to-getherness have a way of turning "warm and cozy" into "listless and grouchy." With the wind howling, the kids bickering, and the walls of the house closing in, it's time to adopt a new strategy for the next blizzard that blows through your town.

First, thaw out those berries you picked back in August, for a cobbler, crisp, or pie that will give everyone a much-needed taste of summer. While the dessert is baking, send the kids on a scavenger hunt through the closets for too-wide neckties, outdated scarves, loose buttons, and other accessories that can be combined into "snowman kits" for use when the storm finally ends. Make several kits, and invite a few nearby families to join you for your own neighborhood winter carnival. While the kids build their last-of-the-season snowmen (and snow-women), you can put together some soup, have some mulled wine or hot apple cider, and calculate the number of days until spring.

Guard against the feelings of isolation that are common during the cold-weather months by entertaining friends and family at home, bearing in mind that winter gatherings needn't be extravaganzas just because they take place indoors. As Kelly Gibson says, "I used to freak out over the menu and how clean my house should be, but hopefully I'm maturing to the point that the food and other stuff is incidental." That's important, because as a minister's wife, Kelly tries to open her home to new congregants at least once a month. "Sharing my home and my kitchen with others needs to be my emphasis. It's a tool I can use to build relationships and invest my life in someone else's."

Unfortunately, along with soups and stews, winter is also the season of colds and viruses, the inevitable result of spending so much time indoors. When seasonal illnesses make the rounds through your family, it helps to have plenty of tasty home remedies on hand, from hot chicken soup to loosen congestion to ice cream to soothe scratchy throats. These endless bouts of cold and flu are truly the times that try mothers' souls, but they're also among the experiences children tend to carry with them into their own adult years. After all, who among us doesn't treasure our memories of having Mom around to fluff our pillows, bring us lunch trays set with ginger ale (don't forget the straw) and macaroni and cheese, and to sit on the edge of our bed for a chat when we start to feel better and boredom sets in. There's an art, I'm convinced, to nursing a sick child through a bout of influenza that is passed on from one generation to the next. Think back to the methods your own mother used to take care of you when you got sick, and tap into these memories to help you and your family weather your next round of flu. Pamper your child with these small treats and comforting rituals, and in no time, you will *both* feel better.

And should you make it all the way through the doldrums of winter without anyone catching a cold, you may even wish to consider letting *everyone* take a pretend "sick day" on a Saturday or Sunday. After all, you *are* sick—sick of winter! Stay home in your pajamas, eat grilled cheese sandwiches and rice pudding (my favorite "sick day" lunch), and watch reruns of the old *I Love Lucy*. Drink warm tea with lemon, take bubble baths, and baby yourselves for a day. Trust me: you will all feel better by morning. Having thus turned the corner, it's time to launch your family's Countdown to Spring. Get out the atlas and plan a family road trip for the first sunny weekend of spring. Fire up the grill and barbecue something for an indoor picnic dinner: hamburgers, hot dogs, even steaks, since grilled food tastes especially good when it's cold out. Wear sunglasses and shorts to your picnic, and serve tall glasses of iced tea and lemonade garnished with mint sprigs, fresh lemon slices, and paper umbrellas.

Savor the closeness of being together during a time of year when, as Nancy Kelleher puts it, "the TV is off, the phone is ignored, the world is gone for a little while, and we talk about us."

And then, blessedly, it will happen, just as you start to think it never will: The first stalks of rhubarb appear in the market. The first crocus pokes jauntily up through the slush. The last icicles lose their grip on the roof and finally crash to their splintery deaths. However it finds us, that first whiff of spring gently rouses us. Our long, languid slumber is over; the mercury rises, and with it, our hopes.

Communities, Neighbors, and Friends

Working mothers like mine were still something of a rarity during the years when I was growing up. The fact that I never felt the least bit shortchanged is a testament to how well my mother managed to juggle her various roles. But part of the credit belongs to our neighbors, the Knudsens, who looked after me when I was sick and had to stay home from school. And while I missed having my mother at home when I was sidelined by a cold or flu, just knowing Mrs. Knudsen was there gave me a sense of well-being, as did the grilled cheese sandwiches she used to make me, in a kitchen that came to feel comfortable to me.

Today, I realize neighbors help to shape our view of the world. Back then, the Knudsens helped me develop a sense of community, as well as an appreciation for the importance of friendship.

Nowadays, with more and more of us living far away from our families, the value of bonding with the people around us is clear. Yet many of us hardly know our own neighbors. In teaching our children not to speak to strangers, in guarding our space in a crowded world, we forget about our need for connection. With so many of us shopping in superstores, commuting to work and lunching alone at our desks, our neighbors are becoming our best hope for restoring our lost sense of community.

Neighbors safeguard our secrets and watch over our homes. They applaud our achievements and ease our defeats. They hold our hands when we're worried and comfort us when we're blue. And over time—and countless potluck dinners shared over legions of picnic tables—new neighbors become old friends and houses become homes.

But given the pace of our lives today, it's not always easy to connect with our neighbors, as Nancy Kelleher and her family discovered when they moved to a small town in western Massachusetts, far away from their relatives in the South. The Kellehers looked forward to forming new friendships to help them all feel more at home. But as the weeks passed with barely a glimpse of their neighbors, the Kellehers' hopes of getting to know them grew dim.

Then, one day when the weather was nice and all the

kids played outside, the moms finally started talking. "We all felt sort of awkward at first, but the kids brought us together," Nancy says. "It was late in the afternoon, and one by one, the fathers started coming home and joining us." Over the next several days, the ice having been broken, "we started relying on each other to watch the kids for a minute while we ran in to get Popsicles or cookies and lemonade. Before you knew it, the lawn chairs were out on a regular basis."

Things really started to gel the day the kids needed a few extra bodies for baseball. "We started playing with them," recalls Nancy. "It was funny, and we started laughing at our styles. The guys were coming home, and they started playing too. Then they all got hungry. Patti, Renee, and I kind of looked at each other and said, 'Well, I have some burgers,' and 'I've got some corn.' Patti had the fixings for salad—the kids were cheering—and we all got excited. I had a few red potatoes and made garlic fries that are still the talk of the neighborhood."

Over the next few weeks, two more potluck dinners followed. After the third, Renee's seven-year-old son, Patrick, looked up from his plate and said, "I love these spurs we have." Renee asked her son what he was talking about and Patrick said, "*You* know. Spur-of-the-moment parties." Two years ago, Renee and her family moved to another town forty-five minutes away, but she and Nancy remain friends, as do their children and husbands.

"Our kids brought us together, but the food made it stick," Nancy says. "We learned so much about our neighbors by the way they shared their families with us at the picnic tables. We learned that our values were the same even though we were from different backgrounds. And for me, those lessons around the table were invaluable in raising our children."

And as the Kellehers and their neighbors found, food and friendships just naturally go together, be it a bagel breakfast shared by young urbanites on a Saturday morning, a fish fry on a suburban cul-de-sac on a Friday night, or a midsummer barbecue in small-town America, where doors still go unlocked and friends drop by to visit.

While we can't all live in stereotypical small towns like these, the spirit of community is alive and well in most places, provided we're willing to coax it out. We can find it not just in our neighborhoods but in our apartment buildings and condo complexes, our churches and charities, our clubs and parks, our institutions and schools. Very often, it just requires a little initiative and a willingness to take a chance that our gestures of friendship will be welcomed and returned.

Preparing special appreciation breakfasts or lunches as a friendly gesture is a great way to take initiative. They are easy to arrange, fun to cook, and greatly enjoyed. Try bringing one to a neighbor celebrating a birthday, or to a mother whose kids are home sick with the flu, or anyone else who deserves to feel special. And the breakfasts needn't be any more elaborate than a quick bread or some muffins wrapped in a pretty cloth napkin and tucked into a basket with some jelly or jam, or an assortment of bagels and flavored cream cheeses with a Thermos of coffee and some juice.

Anne McKay likes to hand a mug of hot soup to the cold crossing guard on duty outside her son's Cleveland school. Whenever Sandy Hay notices someone moving in or out of her Jacksonville, Florida, neighborhood, she brings over a cooler of ice and some soft drinks or a pitcher of tea and some cups, a welcome treat for a family whose refrigerator most likely isn't even plugged in yet.

Gifts of homemade food are a wonderful way to welcome a new family into your neighborhood or building, or to celebrate a housewarming with friends. Try baking a simple cake and taping the recipe to the bottom of a cake plate protected by a layer of plastic wrap, to be revealed only after the cake has been eaten. A fabric ribbon tied around the cake with a single blossom tucked into the bow can make your gift as beautiful as it is tasty.

If you haven't the time to bake something yourself, try one of these combinations: a basket lined with a tea towel and filled with crusty French breads and a bottle of fragrant olive oil; a cheese knife paired with an assortment of cheeses and crackers; a cake or brownie mix with an assortment of wooden spoons and spatulas.

Fine coffees combined with a pair of attractive coffee mugs and a cookie mix are another great gift, as is a selection of teas with some honey and a honey dipper. And a shiny new colander makes a pretty container for a variety of colorful pastas, a chunk of fresh Parmesan cheese, and a container of spaghetti sauce.

When Claudia Moritz noticed the moving van across the street from her South Carolina home, she put together one of the most ingenious welcome-to-the-neighborhood gifts I've ever heard of: a collection of menus from the town's best take-out places, along with a gift certificate and some pretty paper plates and matching napkins. Claudia's new neighbors, who have since become her close friends, were delighted with their gift, and who wouldn't be? I can't imagine a more thoughtful welcome for a family whose pots and pans have yet to be unpacked.

You don't have to be new to the area to appreciate a gift of homemade food from a friend. When Linda Shevchuk was awaiting the arrival of her first baby, she was surprised with a cooler filled with homemade soups and stews frozen in individual serving-size bags. To enjoy a home-cooked meal with her husband after the baby arrived, all Linda needed to do was drop two bags into boiling water for twenty minutes, then slit them open and serve. "I got a lot of great things at my baby shower," recalls Linda, "but that food was the best gift of all." And one that would no doubt be equally appreciated by a college student, a friend with a new job, or anyone living alone.

As these stories show, our children may bring us together, but the food makes it stick. So if it's friendship you're after, start by making it a point to share food with your neighbors: a bumper crop of zucchini from your vegetable patch, some striped bass or rainbow trout from an early morning fishing trip, or a batch of fudge brownies just out of the oven.

Nancy Berns got to know Anda Woodward, her new neighbor, over the hot coals in the Berns's barbecue grill. "My husband took our steaks off the grill one summer night and remarked on how the fire had just reached the perfect temperature," Nancy says. "I noticed Anda on her screened porch and called over to her to feel free to throw her dinner on our grill. She came right over to cook her salmon and the three of us shared a salad I had made. We've been good friends ever since." Learn to recognize these bonding opportunities when they present themselves, or to *create* opportunities when they don't.

When twenty inches of snow fell in suburban Connecticut one weekend, Bob and Gail Storm made their way from house to house, checking on their neighbors and inviting them to a snow party. The Storms had a turkey, someone else had a ham, and several families had the makings of side dishes. Together, they created a meal that fed virtually everyone on the street, along with a fond, lasting memory.

Cook-offs are an easy way to get better acquainted with neighbors, so why not organize one on your block? Choose a simple dish that's part of most people's repertoire—chili, meatloaf, or barbecued ribs all work well—then arrange a potluck supper to go with it. Charge a five-dollar entry fee and use the proceeds for a grand prize for the winner: a cooking class, perhaps, or dinner for two at a restaurant.

If a cooking contest seems too intimidating, how about a sand-castle contest on the beach followed by an old-fashioned clambake, or a snowman-building contest as a prelude to a neighborhood potluck dinner? When the members of Corky Cook's church get together, they often share responsibility for the meal by dividing the alphabet into thirds. Those whose last names begin with the first third of the alphabet bring appetizers or salads, the middle third bring main dishes, and the last third bring desserts. While it may work equally well to have everyone bring whatever they wish, it's been my experience that attendance is better when people are asked to bring something specific.

If you'd like to host a potluck, plan on providing the drinks, plates, cutlery, and napkins, along with the tables and chairs. Furnishing the main course, and asking your guests to bring side dishes and desserts, is another option. When Sandy Hay decided it was high time she got to know her neighbors, for instance, she invited everyone to a fish fry. "In almost every neighborhood we have lived in, folks don't know one another even after many years. Without gathering for a meal, time flies by with the busyness of life. As newlyweds in our first neighborhood, we were amazed at this, so we decided to organize the fish fry. I called the neighbors and discussed what they could bring. We provided the fish and the cook, and used the front of our car covered with a cloth as the serving table. Neighbors who'd hardly spoken to one another before the fish fry hung around and talked into the wee hours of the morning. After that, people would come out in the evening to talk. A neighborhood watch program and much more were created over some fried fish."

Cindi Swett and her neighbors hold a Pig Pickin' Party each May to which every family contributes a small donation and a covered dish to share. "The event starts early Friday evening when preparations for the pig roast begin," Cindi says. "If you like, you can be out all night helping tend the fire. On Saturday, a giant tent covers the whole cul-de-sac and every family is there enjoying the best pork you ever tasted, plus fantastic salads and desserts. Tables are ready and everyone enjoys a relaxing day socializing and catching up with everyone."

Progressive dinners, like the ones Karen Mitch and her neighbors put together, are yet another great way to spend an evening sharing good food with friends without having to cook the entire meal yourself. The dinners feature hors d'oeuvres and drinks at one house, an appetizer or salad at another, a main course at a third, and coffee and dessert at a fourth. The number of courses may vary depending upon the number of couples participating. All you need are three or four who live within walking distance, since strolling from house to house in a group is part of the fun.

Kathy Ames has developed a rather ingenious method of sharing meals with her friends during the four-day camping trips they take every summer from their homes near Sacramento to the northern California lakes. Each family assumes responsibility for one meal during the trip. And while the meals tend to be somewhat gourmet—especially by tent-camping standards—Kathy and her friends find it much easier and more fun to make a single meal for everyone than to plan and cook four days' worth of food for their families alone. The same division of labor would work just as well for families sharing a beach house or renting neighboring cabins in the mountains.

An intimate dinner party for three or four couples can be a great way to entertain friends, provided your schedule and budget allow. Don't let the term "dinner party" scare you; this needn't be a formal event. Lasagna, stew and salad, chili and corn bread, or a baked ham and scalloped potatoes can all qualify as company meals, particularly when you've added a pretty tablecloth, some flowers, and candlelight.

Don't be afraid to experiment with foods at these parties, although I do recommend serving new recipes to your family once or twice before serving them to guests. Keep your recipes simple and try to do as much as possible ahead of time. And don't hesitate to buy some of the foods you'll be serving—unusual bread, say, or a fancy dessert. That way you'll have more time to relax with your guests.

Invite your children to their own fancy dinner the following night, to make up for having sent them to Grandma's the night of the party. Have them wear something special, and let them slip out the back door so they can ring the doorbell and reenter through the front, like real guests. Reuse your centerpiece, flowers, and candles from the night before, and serve them leftover party food if they're old enough to enjoy it. If not, give them something they *will* like, but serve it on your very best china.

While children don't belong at grown-up dinner parties as a rule, they fit right in at the casual outdoor gatherings best held during warm-weather months. Weekend barbecues and brunches are easy and fun to put together. So are afternoon picnics, like the one Sue Moran made for a dozen families last summer. Guests arrived to find Sue's lawn covered by a colorful mosaic of old quilts, which she'd borrowed and pieced together in her backyard. On each quilt was a hamper filled with picnic foods: fried chicken, potato salad, corn bread, and more.

Bluegrass music played in the background as the pic-nickers unpacked their goodies. Sue, in jeans and bare feet, made her way from quilt to quilt with pitchers of lemonade and iced tea, pouring drinks and visiting with her guests, who square-danced well into the night. Along with the summer months, the holidays are a natural time for getting together with large groups of neighbors and friends. But for most of us, the weeks between Thanksgiving and New Year's are also among the year's busiest. With so much to do and so little time to do it, we often find ourselves torn between our responsibilities to our families and our desire to spend time with friends.

The good news is that with careful planning, it is possi-ble to do both. Diane Curtis likes to invite eleven friends to an annual Christmas cookie exchange: Each guest pro-duces thirteen dozen of her favorite cookies, prettily pack-aged in quantities of twelve. Everyone keeps one dozen of the cookies she baked for her own family, and brings the other twelve dozen to the party. One package is given to each of the eleven people assembled, and the remaining dozen is shared over coffee or tea, hot chocolate or sherry. The result: everyone goes home with eleven dozen cook-ies. Their Christmas baking is done, and they've had a chance to socialize in the process! Try the same thing with six friends exchanging casseroles or other one-dish meals, and you'll have a freezer full of options for those busy December evenings spent addressing Christmas cards or shopping or wrapping gifts.

For all its joys, Christmas can be an especially lonely time for those who can't get home to their families. Kelly Godfrey now lives in upstate New York about three hours away from her relatives, but when her husband's career in the Navy found them in Hawaii for Christmas a few years ago, she learned to rely on her neighbors and friends. It was the first time the Godfreys had celebrated the holiday far from their loved ones. "It was strange to wake up to eighty-five-degree weather, and see palm trees instead of evergreens," Kelly recalls. "We opened gifts while on the phone with our family, but of course, it wasn't the same."

But the day brightened up considerably that afternoon, when the Godfreys got together with some of the other officers and their wives who also were far from home for the holidays. "We made a feast together of all our favorite foods, and sat around our friend's huge dining room table while listening to Christmas music. It really made everyone feel not so alone."

If you know several people who aren't able to get home for Christmas or some other holiday—foreign students from a local college, say—you might consider hosting an "orphan's dinner." Reaching out to help others feel less alone is what neighborliness is all about, and we needn't wait for Christmas to do it. Small acts of kindness can go a long way toward creating a family feeling in your apartment building, on your street, or at your children's school. A homemade meal delivered to new parents, a homebound elderly person, or a neighbor just out of the hospital is a gift from the heart that will long be remembered. Inviting a single neighbor to break bread with you and your family, or setting an extra place at your table for a friend whose family is out of town is easy to do, as is baking or buying a cake for someone whose birthday might otherwise go unnoticed.

Hold an evening coffee for your neighbors and invite a knowledgeable resident to discuss some topic or issue that's of interest to you all: financial investments, organic gardening, homeopathic remedies, or flower arranging. Every town has its experts; all it takes is a phone call or two to find them.

Less educational but no less fun are the "Ladies' Nights" Melissa Stromberg and her neighbors enjoy in their small Utah town just north of Salt Lake City. "There are twenty of us in all, and we get together once a month to play games," Melissa says. "The games are mostly silly things, like dice games. The most fun part is being able to get together and socialize without our kids. That and the desserts we eat afterwards. We all have a wonderful time. For a few hours every third Thursday, our biggest concern is finding enough chairs." As Melissa's group can attest, for women with young children, a few hours in the company of grown-ups can be tantamount to a new lease on life.

But you needn't be the mother of a toddler to appreciate the restorative benefits of time spent with neighbors and friends who are our extended family. Close connections with others add texture and meaning to our lives, while reinforcing the notion that we're all a part of something bigger than ourselves. Each of us has something to offer; each of us has something to gain. So what are we waiting for? You bring the burgers. I'll bring the corn.

Holidays

It seems to me every family in America has at least one of the following: a turkey centerpiece fashioned from pinecones dating back to the kids' grade-school days, a grandmother who's so busy waiting on everyone that she's always the last one to come to the table, and a child who annually raids the relish tray for black olives to stick on his fingers.

Furthermore, I'm convinced every family *also* has one of these: a story about the year Mom forgot to turn on the oven to roast the holiday bird; a tale of a turkey accidentally served stuffed with its own bag of giblets; an annual debate over the merits of live versus artificial Christmas trees; and a messy mishap involving an Easter egg that turned out, alas, to be raw.

But for all that, I suspect I'd be hard-pressed to find a

single family that doesn't believe holiday meals are worth all the effort it takes to create them, or that doesn't look forward to these elaborate productions all year long. The rewards, like hungry relatives, come in a steady stream: the scent of celery and onions sizzling away in hot butter; the crisp breezes that blow through the kitchen when we fling open the back door to let out the heat; the sight of our loved ones sitting shoulder-to-shoulder, listening to Grandpa say grace. A whole day to spend with each other, our hearts, mouths, and bellies all full. Such are the singular joys that the holidays bring. And such are the memories that sustain us throughout the years, memories formed at our childhood tables, where lifelong traditions are born.

For most of us, after all, it is our mother's stuffing we serve to our children, along with her cranberry salad and sweet potatoes—the kind with the marshmallows, Suzanne Orr reminds me, and *not* the kind with the weird glaze. "New recipes are fine for any other day," Suzanne says, "but on Thanksgiving, I want those yams with marshmallows, and the Jell-O salad!"

So do I, which is why we Christophers save our experiments for some other day and stick with the tried-and-true favorites that have graced our holiday table for three generations or more. Even now, when I think of Thanksgiving, it's my mother's traditional meal that I picture: her bread stuffing, mashed potatoes and gravy (doesn't everyone believe their mom made the best gravy?), her wonderful fruit salad and pie. And although, sad to say, she is no longer with us, each time I re-create those special dishes, I feel like I'm holding a part of her close.

In the hustle and bustle of the holiday season, it's easy to forget that more than meals, we're also making memories that will stay with our children forever. Actually, I suspect we *do* realize it on some level, given the pressure we heap on ourselves every year to create the kind of holiday dinners that exist only in Norman Rockwell paintings or on the pages of food magazines. If only we could make our meals look like the pictures, we think everything else would be perfect. The children wouldn't bicker, the dinner rolls wouldn't burn, and every bite of white meat would be juicy!

It's a nice thought, but hardly a realistic one. Perfection is, after all, an unattainable goal, and its pursuit only leads to more stress. If we focus on things that matter and take things that don't with a huge grain of salt, we stand a far better chance of enjoying the holidays and creating fond memories for our families—and ourselves.

And besides, some of our best-loved memories involve things that did *not* go according to plan, like the time Shannon Werhanowicz's grandmother left the platter of turkey in the kitchen and served up the carcass instead, or the Christmas Erin McNutt tried to hand-dip some pinecones in gold leaf and wound up with a 14-karat kitchen in the process. As a newlywed, I had my own Thanksgiving disaster, the year I had to work the day after the holiday. Since the family gathering was too far away for us to travel for the day, it meant that Jay and I had to stay home. Rather than roast a whole bird for the two of us, I bought what I thought was a fresh turkey breast. It turned out to be a pressed turkey roll, and any resemblance to actual turkey was purely coincidental.

We all make mistakes, but the biggest mistake of all is to allow the occasional culinary blunder to ruin the holiday with our family. After all, when you stop and think about it, how much of your childhood excitement had to do with the actual meal? Think back to the thrill of watching your uncle's car pull into the driveway and being the first one to shout out, "They're here!" Think back to the sight of the mismatched chairs around the "kids' table" you shared with your siblings and cousins; the rare privilege of drinking from tall crystal glasses just like the grown-ups'; the annual ritual of making a wish with your sister or brother, and hooking your pinkies around the wishbone, each of you angling to snap off the tip. Remember listening to the muffled snores of the uncles who had fallen asleep watching football, or the music of your mother's laughter as she lingered at the table, sipping coffee with your favorite aunt. These are the things that stay with us forever, not whether the dishes were mismatched or the bird overcooked.

How deeply these memories speak to us still: of home and hearth, love and comfort, security and belonging. So powerful are these associations that to this day, whenever she finds herself feeling the slightest bit homesick, Cindi Swett need only fry up a mixture of onions and celery and inhale their familiar aroma to be transported from her Virginia kitchen back to her Pennsylvania roots. It's a ritual that offers a taste of home in much the same way that unpacking her parents' wedding china—blue with a silver pinecone pattern—does for Suzanne Orr.

Suffice it to say that the holidays loom large in the archives of memory, beginning at a very young age. Why else would Karen Mitch sooner endure her kids' teasing than update her Thanksgiving centerpiece—a pilgrim she made in first grade? How else could we account for Betsy Barr's fondest recollection of her childhood holidays: eating scraps of raw dough as her grandmother cut out the rolls.

For Nancy Kelleher, who grew up with five siblings, the

big moment always came *after* the feast: waiting to see who got to "crumb" the table with her mother's silver crumber, a treasured utensil brought out only on special occasions. Similarly, the highlight of the Werhanowicz family's Thanksgiving consists of blowing out the dinner candles after everyone's finished eating, an honor that always goes to the two youngest guests—a clever strategy, since "this usually helps them stay patiently in their seats til the end, rather than running around while everyone else is finishing," Shannon Werhanowicz says.

Another tradition you could begin that will create great memories and also help the day go more smoothly is to provide little "treat cups" at each child's place, filled with M&Ms or some other sweet that's not to be touched til the end of the meal. Or having a kids' "tablecloth" of white butcher paper and short glasses filled with colorful crayons. Of course, that's assuming we're able to make room for them amid all the platters and bowls!

As an alternative, plan to come to the table armed with a selection of quiet activities. When the youngsters are finished eating, replace their dirty plates with storybooks, puzzles, or toys. Or have them work on a project together, like the "Thankful Turkey" Zachary Norden created with his cousins a few years ago, with each construction paper "feather" representing a blessing, a reminder of Thanksgiving's true purpose.

However it's expressed, gratitude deserves a place at our Thanksgiving tables, for this is a day to feel blessed—to feel *prosperous*—even for those who are not. As Edna Abrams says of her early Thanksgivings, "I know now that we were very poor during those Depression years, but I did not know it then. Our traditions were very rich, and I felt the same. I still do." Indeed, we can *all* feel like millionaires on Thanksgiving, simply by gazing at the faces of our loved ones and rejoicing at being together. Try joining hands and taking a moment before dinner to share what you're most thankful for, a custom that's been in my family for at least half a century and one that never fails to make us feel graced.

It may take a more concerted effort to stay focused on the spiritual aspects of Christmas or Chanukah, given the rampant commercialism that creeps into the season a bit earlier with each passing year. Like most people who came of age in the decades before high-tech toys, I remember my early Christmases as having been relatively modest, yet infused with a magic all their own. To say I looked forward to Christmas morning would be an understatement; I once snuck down to the tree under cover of darkness to unwrap—then *rewrap*—my gifts!

Christmas was always my favorite day of the year, but it was just that: a *day*, not a four-week extravaganza! Back then, the decorations and cards didn't appear until well after Thanksgiving; nowadays, it seems, we all start seeing red the day after Halloween! Mind you, it's not that I don't still love Christmas. It's just that I'm having to work a bit harder to preserve its true meaning, and I suspect you and your families are, too.

There's not much one can do about the glut of catalogs, commercials, and store displays aimed at the youngest consumers, but we *can* remind our children that Christmas, Chanukah, and Kwaanza are not supposed to be about receiving gifts or the amount of money you've spent on one.

To get the season off to an altruistic start, organize an outing with friends and neighbors and their children to decorate doors at a nursing home. Along with promoting sound values, you'll be brightening up the holidays for the patients. Decorate the inside of the doors as well as the outside, to encourage residents to keep their doors open. Pull out and help polish menorahs—place them around the common rooms. Give a prize to the decorator who comes up with the most original ideas.

Back on the home front, you can greatly cut down the annual chorus of "I want this! I want that!" by taping an envelope to the refrigerator for every member of the family. Whenever anyone sees something he or she wants for the holidays, have them jot down the name and a brief description of the coveted item on a slip of paper and place it in the proper envelope. When it's time to shop, have everyone empty his or her envelope and prioritize the items inside to put a stop to the scrambling for gift ideas.

While your children are busy listing their choices, sit down and make a list of your own of all the chores large and small that need to be done prior to the holiday celebration: retrieving decorations from the basement or attic; wrapping gifts; addressing cards; untangling lights, etc. A month or so before the holiday, cut up the list into individual tasks, place them in a hat, and summon your clan to the table. Break out the ribbon candy, eggnog, or some other holiday treat, and pass the hat until every last chore's been assigned. Then, as long as you have their attention, schedule a family gift-making workshop for a weekend in early December.

Gingerbread, sugar cookies, or fudge packed in pretty tins or fabric-covered boxes make ideal gifts for the teachers, coaches, and other important adults in your kids' lives. So do homemade tea breads wrapped in foil and tied with bright holiday ribbon, fragrant herb vinegars in collectible glass bottles, and sweet or savory spreads in crocks, all with their recipes attached. Make pomanders out of oranges and whole cloves, or mix fragrant leaves, dried flowers, herbs and spices, and aromatic oils to make potpourri. Wrapped in cellophane and tied with ribbon, these make beautiful, inexpensive gifts for babysitters, friends, neighbors, or relatives.

With holiday music playing softly in the background, your children will feel like Santa himself as they decorate cookies or frost cupcakes to bring to a children's hospital, or bake biscuits for the dogs at an animal shelter. Projects like these really bring home to children the true satisfaction of giving, and they're a great way to spend quality time with your family doing something besides fighting the crowds.

As the grand finale to gift-making day, treat your family to a driving tour of your community's Christmas lights. Preheat the car and drive off in your pajamas and bathrobes with holiday music on the tape player. Come home to hot chocolate and Christmas cookies, or some other festive dessert.

Another great way to reinforce the joy of giving in your children is to help them go through their closets and toy boxes a week or two before Christmas for clothes that no longer fit and games, dolls, and toys they no longer play with. Throw out any items that are beyond repair, and wash and refurbish the rest. Take your children to the library to donate their old books, and help them donate toys and clothing to charity. Christa Jamison's twin daughters are only three, but when they get a bit older, she plans to ask them each to donate one of their presents to an under-privileged child in the community. These activities teach children about the meaning of the holiday and help them feel good about themselves in the process.

Jewish families can accomplish much the same thing by doing a *mitzvah*—good deed—for each of the eight days of Chanukah. Shoveling a slippery sidewalk, reading a story to a younger sibling, running an errand for an elderly neighbor, or carrying grocery bags in from the car are but a few possibilities, but anything that makes life a little easier for someone else serves the purpose, while enhancing the doer's self-esteem.

Making room at your table for someone who'd other-wise be alone is another way to emphasize the true mean-ing of Christmas. Several years ago, Diane Tejeda decided to set an extra place to signify that a stranger was wel-come. "My family thought I was nuts," Diane says, "but now, whenever I set that place, it is always filled." Christa Jamison, whose husband is in the Air Force, opens her house to fellow servicemen and women whose duties prevent them from going home for Christmas din-ner. Families in college and university towns could do the same for foreign students, or anyone else who's unable to get home.

However you and your family choose to do it, try to make this the year you reclaim the season's true spirit with small acts of kindness: invite someone to share a worship service or a concert; share homemade gifts from your kitchen; add an extra person or two at your table. Make this the year you don't go into debt, gain ten pounds, or become hopelessly overextended; the year your family discovers that simple is best. Celebrate the end as well as the start of the holiday season by having a party as you *undress* the tree. Sing Christmas songs one last time, sip some punch, and polish off the cookies in one last hurrah that will help everyone cope with the inevitable post-Christmas letdown.

And then ring in the New Year together, with a menu chosen to bring you good luck: black-eyed peas from the South; pork and sauerkraut from the North; a whole fish served with both head and tail, a Chinese custom that ensures a good ending to the old year and a good beginning to the new. As a little added insurance, be sure to serve something besides the whole fish, since your kids may refuse to go anywhere near it! Dine by the light of two bayberry candles, letting them burn themselves out—another time-honored New Year's tradition.

Be sure to open the front door at midnight to let the old year out and the new one in, the way my sisters and I always did, having whiled away the evening making popcorn and fudge. Come back to the table to share your resolutions, predictions, and dreams for the future over one last fancy holiday dessert. Jot down your predictions and put them away, to be read at the table next year. Make a family resolution, along with your individual ones. Resolve to spend one day a month helping others, and make a list of the ways you can do so. On the first of each month, take turns choosing a good deed from your list and scheduling a time to go do it.

If you're anything like me, you probably greet the second of January with mixed feelings. On the one hand, it's something of a relief to have the holidays over for another year; to go back to work, school, and the familiar routine—not to mention lighter and healthier meals! On the other hand, the house always looks so empty after the holiday things are safely tucked away, and knowing we face three dark, cold winter months doesn't make the chore any easier. But just when we think it'll never be spring, along comes Easter Sunday, with its message of hope and renewal.

A black-and-white photo of me in my front yard taken years ago captures the paradoxical nature of this holiday perfectly. The lawn appears dead in the photo, as are all the bushes, and the tree beside me is scrawny and bare. I'm wearing patent-leather party shoes and white anklets, and my new gingham dress is all but smothered by my dark winter coat. A new white purse is slung over my shoulder, and a thousand-watt grin lights my face. You can practically smell the chocolate bunny on my breath.

What's not to love about Easter, with its fragrant bulbs, gaudy hats, pastel eggs, and baby chicks. It's a visual feast for eyes starving for color, and the best excuse to hop out of bed since December. As my mother indulged me, so have I indulged both my daughters, with Easter baskets, new outfits, colored eggs, candy—even a real, live Easter bunny that became part of the family. Our early church service is one of the year's loveliest, with music that's truly heavenly. Sometimes we even come home to a clove-studded ham with all the trimmings, just as I did on that spring Sunday years ago.

Early spring is also the time of Passover, the joyous eight-day Jewish holiday that celebrates the Israelites' deliverance from slavery and their journey to the promised land. It is a time of celebration and remembrance, story-telling and song, centered around a special Seder ceremony that takes place at the table. A Seder is both a religious service and a ritualized meal in which certain foods are used to retell the Passover story. Passover cooking differs from that of the rest of the year in that leavening agents are strictly forbidden, which is why Jews substitute matzoh and matzoh meal for bread and flour during the holiday. Indeed, preparing for Passover involves a thorough spring house cleaning in which every crumb of leavened food is removed.

For Leigh Sims and her family, the Passover Seder is an eagerly awaited event to be shared with two dozen or more relatives and friends. "Our table is usually a rainbow of colors and cultures," says Leigh. "We always have the traditional foods that are associated with the holiday: matzoh ball soup, gefilte fish, chopped liver, and of course, pot roast." Other traditional treats include roast chicken or brisket, with macaroons, honey cake, or sponge cake for dessert.

Whether Passover or Easter is a religious holiday for your family or simply a harbinger of the warm weather to come, why not mark winter's end at your table with a dinner that celebrates spring. Place several small flowering plants in a basket for the centerpiece, or place flowering branches of forsythia, cherry, or quince in front of your children and commission some original art. Set a plain straw hat, ribbon, artificial flowers and fruit at each place, and make your own bonnets to wear during dinner. Serve new potatoes, asparagus, and leg of spring lamb, with strawberry shortcake for dessert. Have an Easter egg or scavenger hunt, go for a bike ride, and eat something—*anything*—chocolate.

Savor the moments you spend at the table surrounded by people you love. Commit them to memory—store them deep in your archives—so that you can relive them at will, because these special days are the jewels in life's crown. And while we may not fully appreciate them at the time, racing back and forth with our platters and bowls, we look back on them later through the softening filter of time as the very best days of our lives.

As Nancy Kelleher says of her childhood Thanksgivings, "Someone always spilled, someone always cried, the mothers never got to eat, but we would always laugh and have a great time." Precisely. The holidays are joyous, chaotic, exhausting, delicious, warm-hearted, exciting, and fun. So dust off the card tables, break out the olives, and scour the attic for that silly centerpiece you made so long ago. Happy holidays! May yours be merry and bright.

The Children's Hour

As a little girl, I knew better than to get in my mother's way when she was trying to get a meal on the table. My mother was, after all, a busy woman with a full-time job and five hungry people to feed. So from the time she got home to the time we sat down to supper, she hadn't a moment to lose as she sped around the kitchen, her hands a blur as she chopped, seasoned, and stirred. Like my sisters before me, I learned to make myself scarce; it was simply a matter of survival.

But I also recall those occasions when we worked on a project together, like the wonderful cinnamon rolls we made for breakfast on holidays and special occasions. I would kneel on a kitchen chair, my arms dusted with flour and one of Mother's aprons encircling me. It'd be just the two of us, baking together. The warmth of the oven, the gentleness of her tone, and the nose-prickling aroma of hot cinnamon all blended to transform our modest little kitchen into a soothing and magical place where I felt wonderfully snug and secure. If only our kitchen had been a bit bigger—big enough for both my sisters to join us.

Happily, times have changed, and today's kitchens have been expanded to accommodate not just the big people who cook in them, but the little ones who like to hang around and watch, with peanut butter on their breath and a spatula in their hands. Actually, the concept of kitchen as playroom probably goes back many years, to the first resourceful grandmother who discovered that in a pinch, plastic bowls and wooden spoons make great toys. She was undoubtedly the very same woman who initiated the practice of handing out nuggets of raw dough and batter-covered spoons to children too impatient to await the cookies and cake. Not surprisingly, kids have been loitering in kitchens ever since.

As long as they're already in there, why not go ahead and put them to work? Kitchens make ideal classrooms, and smart parents know that the feelings of pride and accomplishment in even the littlest cooks can launch a lifetime of healthy habits, and a lifelong appreciation for the pleasures of sharing food with our families. Cooking is a great way to bond with your children, and the warm, loving feelings this shared experience engenders can come in very handy during those tough teenage years.

Learning to cook also can help the most finicky child broaden his or her culinary horizons, since the thought of eating Mom's vegetables is nowhere near as exciting as the prospect of stir-frying one's own, particularly while wearing a child-size apron and a genuine chef's hat like the ones that are available from restaurant supply houses. Pick up some chopsticks and fortune cookies while you're there, and you'll have the makings of a Chinese-style feast, to say nothing of a marvelous photo opportunity.

Be sure to invite sons as well as daughters into your kitchen, for the size of the room isn't all that has changed. When I was a girl, kitchens were viewed as women's places, and it was a rare man who took his turn at the stove. But these days, basic food preparation is considered a life skill that everyone needs. Eating is, after all, something we all do, so why shouldn't cooking be, too? More and more couples are cooking together or taking turns fixing meals for each other. And people are marrying later—therefore living on their own a lot longer. So, more men are cooking than ever, and it's never too early to start.

Being comfortable in the kitchen is the logical first step, and it's one even a toddler can take, by playing with wooden spoons and food storage containers side-by-side with you while you cook, or by keeping you company while you wash the dishes.

Once a child is old enough to actually start helping, as opposed to playing nearby while you work, it's worth investing in an apron to protect him or her from the inevitable splashes and splatters that are bound to accompany those initial efforts. While we're on the subject of safety, it goes without saying that young children should be kept away from sharp knives and hot stoves. Be sure to turn pot handles toward the middle or back of the stove, and also keep hot cookware and hot foods out of reach. Mop up water or other spills promptly, before anyone can slip and fall. Always pull a child's long hair back into a bun or ponytail before tackling any cooking or baking project. And make it clear to young children who are learning to cook that *all* appliances and utensils are strictly off-limits unless a grown-up is present to help.

When it comes to cooking with kids, Kathy Ames is an expert, having run her own day care center for more than twenty years. With up to eight kids in attendance, the youngest of whom is just two, Kathy is an expert at safety as well, and insists that the children all watch from their seats when she's cooking on top of the stove. Over the course of the school year, she and her students make applesauce and apple pies, mashed, fried, and baked potatoes, and popcorn and corn on the cob, along with hot chocolate, gingerbread houses, and pumpkin pies. They also dip whole fish in paint to make fish prints, make scratch-and-sniff pictures out of Kool-Aid, fingerpaint with pudding, and decorate sugar cookies on holidays. "If there's a food to go with the subject I'm teaching, we make it," says Kathy, who believes early childhood is the perfect time to start cooking with children, since little ones love nothing better than to help.

I agree, having found that with adult supervision a three-year-old can stand on a sturdy stool or chair and wash and tear lettuce, open simple packages, and stir ingredients, while an older sibling or parent holds the bowl (and the chair!). A mini-muffin tin and some Play-Doh or a scrap of bread dough and a countertop can provide an hour of fun for a very young child. With Stacey Schrock's guidance and a just-add-water cake mix, her three-year-old is already producing simple desserts. Instant pudding is another great way to launch a cooking career, since all you need is a whisk and a bowl. And there are few things in life that are more satisfying for a precocious preschooler than cracking eggs for an omelette or cake.

The littlest things mean a lot to young children, as Suzie Peterson likes to point out. Her kids, ages two and four, love to make juice in the morning. "They work on their counting skills by adding the right amount of water, and they are instantly gratified when the juice is done and they get to have a glass," says Suzie, who also lets them take turns whisking the batter for weekend breakfasts of pancakes or waffles. Karen Mitch's seven-year-old daughter, Emily, and five-year-old son, Charlie, have been helping her in the kitchen as long as she can remember, beginning with pancakes and cookies. "Over the years, my son has actually taken over the 'little chef' role in the house," Karen says. "He's right there when he hears me cooking or the mixer starts. And only *he* can crack the eggs. For five years old, he's a pretty darn good egg cracker! My daughter does step in every once in a while, but usually for samples."

Both children like to make their own sandwiches. "It helps them appreciate what I do three times a day for the whole family," Karen says. Two of Jeanell Climer's daughters, ages four and two, take great pride in helping their aunt make her famous potato salad by measuring and mixing the ingredients. "Once they are older, they will be allowed to help cook the meal," Jeanell says. In the meantime, they are learning to set the table and clear their own dishes, something every school-age child should do.

For most preschoolers, ice cream sundaes, parfaits, and floats—soda with a scoop or two of ice cream—are simple to make and delicious to eat. So are peanut-butter-and-jelly sandwiches, which can be transformed into something a bit fancier with the help of a cookie cutter. Little ones might also enjoy fixing an "alphabet lunch," by choosing three letters of the alphabet—*e, f, g,* for example—and helping put together a meal using foods that start with those three letters: egg salad, fruit cocktail, grape juice.

Small children love to build their own "funny face" salads by using raisins, sliced apple, celery or carrot pieces, curly lettuce, etc., to transform drained canned peach or pear halves into faces or figures. Help them work on their hand-eye coordination by threading chunks of strawberry, pineapple, and banana onto wooden skewers to make fruit kebabs. Slice-and-bake sugar cookies are another fun decorating project for kids this age. "The trick is to keep plenty of kid-friendly toppings on hand, like colored sprinkles, sugars, red-hots, and so on," says Joyce Madson, whose kids are inveterate decorators.

Portioning dough on a cookie sheet or baking stone, tossing a salad, spreading tomato sauce and mozzarella on an English muffin or French bread to make pizza, and combining wet and dry ingredients in a bowl all help to further a child's coordination, not to mention his or her self-esteem. From simple breakfasts to sweet bedtime snacks, I strongly believe that more opportunities to boost little egos can be found in the kitchen than in any other room in the house.

First grade is a good time to start teaching kids about healthy eating by introducing them to the basic food groups, as well as some of the important vitamins and minerals contained in foods. Take them along when you go grocery shopping. Without getting overly technical, show them how to evaluate fruits and vegetables for freshness and quality, making it a hands-on experience. Encourage them to smell and touch produce, if possible; to recognize the difference between a peach that is hard and odorless and one that's flavorful and ripe. First-graders are also able to help put together their own school lunches, such as sliced apple and peanut butter sandwiches, or tuna salad and lettuce tucked into whole wheat pita bread.

When time allows, invite them into the kitchen, perhaps on a weekend afternoon, to tackle a project of their choosing. Pizza, quesadillas, chili, popovers and muffins are among the many kid-friendly possibilities. I still recall the pride I took in my first batch of cookies, baked under my sister Donna's watchful eye, and the glow on my daughter Kelley's face each time she pulled a tiny cake out of her E-Z Bake oven. It's the very same expression I now see on the faces of the twenty or so ten-year-olds who invade our basement every December for a gingerbread house–decorating party given by my daughter Julie for her Sunday school class.

While all children can benefit from the confidence that comes with acquiring these new cooking skills, kids who struggle with physical or developmental challenges may gain the most from their kitchen adventures. Remember that cooking involves not just math, but also reading, co-ordination, following directions, cleaning up after your-self—even a bit of basic chemistry and physics. Then there's the economics of grocery shopping, the impor-tance of good nutrition, and the organizational skills needed to follow a recipe. Simply helping a child get into the habit of making sure all the necessary ingredients are on hand before starting a project reinforces the impor-tance of planning ahead and of thinking things through step by step.

Just remember to keep the projects simple and the

kitchen tools basic to increase the odds of a triumph and lessen the chance of a mess. As Theresa McMahon suggests, "You want to make things achievable, nonfrustrating, and fun." Close your eyes to the chaos and let them experiment from time to time. And try not to criticize the results.

Because the proof isn't just in the pudding, in this case; it's also in the pudding-maker himself. Just ask Sandy Hay, whose son, Charles, has been her right hand in the kitchen for more than a dozen years now, having mashed, stirred, and mixed with both parents ever since he was in diapers. Charles was just two when he pushed the little girls next door out of their play kitchen, and the Hays have the photos to prove it.

That Christmas, Charles got his own play kitchen, but he soon made it clear he preferred the real thing. At eight, he appeared in his parents' bedroom one morning with a nine-by-thirteen-inch pan in his hand and an ear-to-ear grin on his face. "Who says we can't have cake for breakfast?" asked Charles. Certainly neither of his parents! "We sat on the bed and had cake for breakfast," says Sandy. "He was so proud, and it was a great cake."

By eleven, Charles was cooking dinner for his family, and selling homemade brownies and lemonade at his mother's garage sales. He's fourteen now, an accomplished baker who likes to bring his fresh cookies to parties and other gatherings—it helps break the ice and boost his self-confidence in new social situations. As an added benefit, Sandy reports, "We get along better when we are cooking together. It's a great time for the two of us to talk." What began as a hobby already has evolved into a passion, and may one day become something more. Charles plans to attend cooking camp next summer, and he hopes to eventually work as a chef.

Learning to cook has greatly improved Charles's self-image, just as it enhanced my own years ago. I still remember so vividly the pride and accomplishment I felt as a girl having produced my first batch of cookies. For the first time in my young life, I felt accomplished—and my self-esteem soared off the charts. Instead of dwelling on things that were hard for me, I began to focus on things I did well—and all because of those chocolate chip cookies.

I've never outgrown my need for positive reinforcement, and I'm convinced nobody ever really does. So, once your kids have learned the basics—simple cooking techniques and safety—you might try sparking their imaginations by teaching them the importance of presentation, eye-appeal, and all the other niceties that can help make any meal seem a little more special. As a teenager, I soaked these things up like a sponge, paying close attention to how Maxine Christopher, Jay's mother, folded napkins, arranged flowers, or garnished plates with fresh herbs—she was great with these decorator touches. Older children often consider these tasks great fun to do—my daughters have always loved making centerpieces out of cut flowers, weeds, seedpods, and other natural materials. Invite your kids to scour the cupboard and yard for supplies with which to create special settings. Borrow a book on napkin-folding from the library, and have each member of the family learn one technique. Take turns adding this finishing touch to your table for special dinners on weekend nights.

Serving dinner in the dining room, complete with candles, will encourage your children to put their new culinary skills to use. Teaching kids the proper placement of silverware and the purpose of each fork and spoon demystifies so-called fine dining and helps children feel comfort-

able in a wider range of social situations. You needn't prepare a fancy feast to accomplish this—all it takes is a
change of setting to make kids aware of the "specialness" of
a meal—but you may wish to "go formal" by using the
good dishes and pouring milk or juice into stemware.

Older children may also enjoy the challenge of planning a meal and shopping for the ingredients, a great way
to teach them about basic household economics and menu
planning. Start with a supermarket circular to see what's
on sale, then point out appropriate recipes. Encourage your
child to invite a friend to share this special meal with your
family, or perhaps to throw a dinner party of her own. Stay
behind the scenes as the "sous" chef and chief bottle-
washer, and let your son or daughter play host. Talk about
an ego boost!

At eleven and seven, Kathy Ames's sons are already taking turns planning a week's worth of meals at a time. Kathy
sometimes provides a theme, such as vegetarian foods or
ethnic dishes, to get her boys started. Other times, she
hands them a supermarket ad and limits them to foods that
are on sale. "After the menu is made, they help with various preparations: cleaning produce, measuring, chopping,
slicing, grating, mashing, cooking, and setting the table,"
Kathy says. "I believe that all these things have given my
children more self-confidence, managing skills, money and
math skills, and a sense of nutritional values—things

they'll need throughout their lives." And by the time her sons are ready to live on their own, these life skills will be second-nature to them both.

But even more important will be all the memories of their time in the kitchen with Mom. For Diane Shephard, who grew up with nine sisters and one brother, "my favorite memory is of helping my mother in the kitchen. I learned some wonderful things. My mother taught me with such patience. I learned more at the kitchen table than I did anywhere else. Having so many sisters, getting to spend some special time with my mother in the kitchen was heaven."

That isn't to say cooking with Dad can't be every bit as memorable for children, as Elinor Sossong's kids discovered last Mother's Day, when Elinor made an unusual request. Instead of store-bought gifts or a meal at a restaurant, she asked her husband and three children to cook for the day. "There was one condition," she recalls. "They had to enjoy it and have fun—no fighting!" It seemed a tall order, given that her husband, Fred, barely cooks, and his kitchen staff's ages were three, five, and eight.

As the oldest, Gregory Sossong was designated the official recipe reader and chopper; his sisters, Kimberly and Carolyn, were the "stirrers." Elinor sat at the dining room table with her feet propped up watching the show. It was better than anything they could have bought her, as was the dinner they made her. Her favorite "mental snapshot" of that Mother's Day: the sight of her husband playfully spraying whipped cream directly into the children's mouths. With their heads tipped back and their mouths opened wide to receive it, they looked to their mother "just like baby birds."

As all five Sossongs discovered that day, no gift is more special than the one you make yourself, with your own hands and plenty of love. What better lesson to teach to our children, and what better way for them to learn it? Yes, it *would* be much easier to cook by yourself, but think of all that your kids would miss out on. The opportunity to bond with your children, to teach them new skills and enhance their self-esteem is worth a few dirty dishes and a bit of spilled milk. Before you get started, of course, you'll want to stock up on those ingredients that can't be found in any store but that are crucial when cooking with kids: Tolerance. Patience. And above all, good humor. Spills happen; that's why God made wipes. Bad results happen, too— even to the most seasoned chefs. There's a valuable lesson to be learned here, as well: Everyone makes mistakes, so don't worry. The good news is that even "mistakes" can taste good!

So tie on your apron and roll up your sleeves. Summon your kids to the kitchen to toss their first salad or stir their first stew. Let them crack eggs for French toast or sprinkle cheese on a pizza. Spend a rainy afternoon together baking some cookies, the kind with the big chocolate kisses on top. See the pride in their eyes as Dad tastes their creation, and savor the moment along with the treat. Life just doesn't get any sweeter.

Summer Pleasures

Ah, summer. Even in January's dark depths, the mere thought makes us smile, for it is filled with the promise of pleasures to come: red, ripe tomatoes, hot buttered corn, creaking porch swings, and salty sea breezes, to say nothing of lightning bugs, Queen Anne's lace, and the timeless summer symphony of hissing lawn sprinklers, chirping crickets, and banging screen doors.

To a child walking home on the last day of school, the stretch between June and September seems endless. But to a grown-up forced to squeeze three months' worth of fun in the sun into a series of much-too-short weekends, summer's pleasures are fleeting, and no opportunity to enjoy them can afford to be overlooked. On the contrary; the true sunworshiper is forever seeking new ways to incorporate that "vacation" feeling into his or her workday world, be it by breakfasting on the deck at the first light of day, or by barbecuing Monday night's chicken alongside Sunday's grilled steaks.

This is, after all, the one time of year when we needn't be tied to our ovens; when our "tables" can be anything from a quilt in a meadow to a blanket on the beach, and our suppers can truly be moveable feasts. Now's our chance to reclaim the Great Outdoors as our own private dining room—ants, birds, and squirrels notwithstanding—with picnics and barbecues, campfires, and clambakes.

For most of us, summer's long, lazy days are perfect for casual entertaining and spur-of-the-moment get-togethers featuring light, easy menus reflecting our mood. Paper plates replace china and sparkling salads replace roasts when the mercury climbs and the seashore beckons. It is time once again to pick peaches, eat lobsters, toast marshmallows, and slurp Popsicles. And to somehow find ways to soak up enough of these bright, sunny days to carry us through the cold months ahead, when the taste of fresh raspberries warmed by the sun will be but a fond, fading memory.

Of all summer's myriad flavors, it is that one—the sweet, tangy taste of fresh raspberries—that transports me back through the decades to my parents' cottage near Lake

Michigan's shore, where we vacationed for a month every summer. For those four idyllic weeks, we slept in bunk beds and lived in bathing suits, paddling around in the lake in inner tubes, building castles in the sand, and eating our fill of berries from the local farms that dotted the landscape. After dinner, we would walk slowly back to the beach with our ice cream cones clutched in our fists to watch the sun slip behind the lake in one last blaze of glory, a nightly spectacle that made us forget about TV. That was a very long time ago, but I still happily head for the lake with my family to escape the heat during summer's dog days, as does Sue Allshouse, who spends sultry weekends with her husband and kids at her father-in-law's cottage on Devil's Lake.

"There are usually eleven or twelve people there, so food preparation is definitely involved," Sue says. "Most often, a summer meal is a cookout, with steaks, hamburgers, sweet corn, and salads filled with luscious garden vegetables. The family eats outside on the deck and Grandpa delights in hearing all the giggles from the children. Summer is the time of year for us when our batteries get charged—sort of a rejuvenation to help us get through the long, cold Michigan winter. It is the happiest time for our family as we spend many hours together relaxing and enjoying nature."

Summer is a great season for starting new family traditions, since the extra hours of sunlight give us long days with our loved ones, and the blissfully warm weather encourages us to venture outside together. One of the most rewarding ways to experience the wonders of nature with your children is by planting a vegetable garden. Connie Barzona found this out when she and her grandchildren planted tomatoes, cucumbers, string beans, and sweet corn in Connie's backyard. "They are so thrilled to watch it grow and then to be able to eat it," Connie says.

The little ritual of walking out to the garden to gather the vegetables or flowers helps us stay in touch, in a small way, with the cycles of nature and the soil from which our food comes. It saddens me to see each generation becoming a little bit farther removed from these kinds of experiences. Heaven forbid our children grow up thinking tomatoes come from cans—or without ever tasting a "real" tomato, as opposed to the red rubber balls found in markets in February! If this matters to you and your family, I urge you to grow something—anything—edible, if only a cherry tomato plant on a windowsill, lest you run the risk of losing touch with this most basic reality.

If you do decide to roll up your sleeves and get out the hoe, you and your loved ones will be richly rewarded—not just with homegrown tomatoes, but with the sense of wonder your children experience upon watching the seedling grow into a fruit. Several years ago, Teresa Blake helped her stepdaughter put in tomato plants for the first time. "The first tomato was always reserved for Daddy and the second was always for her," recalls Teresa, who says the ritual has developed into a much-loved summer tradition for all three of them.

There's an added benefit to growing your own produce, as Lisa Walker points out. The child who helps tend the family garden is far less likely to refuse to eat vegetables. Such is the case for eight-year-old Chip Walker, who normally turns his nose up at anything green, but who has made an exception for his mom's homegrown cukes. "Somehow, the cucumbers we grow are delicious to him," Lisa says. "What a treat it is for me to see him come back for more."

For older children, like Sharon Burke's daughter, having

a whole row of the garden all to themselves to design and plant, weed and harvest can be a wonderfully satisfying adventure. A word of caution, however, for first-time gardeners: Don't make the same classic mistake Sharon's parents did the summer her family moved to the country, having decided to live off the land. "Little did we know that every zucchini plant didn't produce just *one* zucchini, and each tomato plant didn't produce just *one* tomato," Sharon recalls. "We planted close to a half-acre of each!"

Not coincidentally, that was also the summer the Burkes learned how to can—producing what Sharon describes as enough stewed tomatoes and homemade spaghetti sauce to feed their entire New Hampshire town for a year! Despite all the work—or because of it—Sharon recalls that long-ago summer as one of the best of her life. She still proudly upholds her mother's longstanding tradition of putting far too many zucchini and tomato plants in her garden, and, like her mom, she still devotes the better part of August to the ritual of canning the surplus.

Sharon also plants marigolds in honor of her brown-thumbed mother, whose attempts to grow flowers on the family farm were disastrous—*except* for the marigolds. I remember when petunias and marigolds were the quintessential summer blooms, but nowadays, there's a far greater variety of flowers available that are highly adaptable and simple to grow. A small cutting garden is easy to care for, and I think it's well worth the investment to be able to dress up the table with colorful arrangements of zinnias, snapdragons, and daisies.

If you don't have the time or space for a garden, *do* take your children to a local farmers' market or pick-your-own orchard or melon patch. Let them see where food comes from and meet some of the hardworking farmers who produce it. "My daughter loves to help pick out fruit, to smell the cantaloupe and feel the peaches," Sue Allshouse says. The sight of fat watermelons lying in the fields, bushes laden with blueberries, or plump ears of corn on the stalk gives kids a much greater appreciation for the effort involved in bringing food from the field to the table, something we all tend not to think about in the course of our daily lives.

Once you've picked your fair share of berries, set some aside for your own homemade jellies or jams, an easy project that fascinates children. Years ago, Leslie Norden and her four sisters routinely spent part of their summers swarming over the berry patches of Michigan, dutifully sampling fruit from each plant before picking, as per their father's instructions. While the girls picked, their mother prepared canning jars in the kitchen of their summer cottage. The actual cooking and processing was a highly anticipated event that "would take two whole days in the kitchen," recalls Leslie. "You had to be careful not to slam the door or the jars would crack." But just imagine how fragrant that simmering jam must have smelled!

The family jam supply, which had to last til the following summer, was as closely guarded as Fort Knox by Leslie's dad. "When I went away to college, my mom handed me a strawberry jam and then a cherry to pack away to remind me of home. Unfortunately, my dad was less willing to share, and so the handling of the jam became a secret mission each time I went back to school," Leslie recalls. "This tradition has been passed down to me and my sisters." Jams, jellies, pickles, and other home-canned goodies also make great Christmas, Chanukah, or Kwaanza gifts, so you may wish to double the recipe in order to share this wonderful taste of summer with friends, the way Leslie and her sisters always do.

Decorate your canning jars by tying a raffia bow around the lid, with a dried orange or lemon slice threaded through the raffia and a whole cinnamon stick tucked into the bow. (Orange or lemon slices can be air-dried or placed in a 200-degree oven.) Cut small rounds of fabric with pinking shears and use to cover the jar lids. Or attach a small bunch of dried herbs or flowers with a paper ribbon for another finishing touch that can turn an ordinary jar of preserves or flavored vinegar into a beautiful gift.

As soon as your jams, pickles, and preserves have been processed, it's time to turn off the oven and fire up the barbecue, because nothing says "summer" like the taste of grilled foods, at least not in my family's opinion. From the simplest hamburgers to the most elaborate mixed grill, there are very few foods that don't benefit from a brief rendezvous with hot coals—not just meats, but vegetables, fruits, even breads, all taste better when cooked out-of-doors, and you'll be spared both the hot, steamy kitchen and all the dirty pots and pans. Use the extra time, usually reserved for cleanup, to sit at the picnic table a while longer with the family.

Virtually anything that can be cooked in an oven or on top of a burner can also be made on a grill, a camp stove, or over an open fire, so why not experiment a bit on your next family camping trip? Carol Olson, an inveterate camp cook, turns out everything from lasagna to cobblers to breakfast hash in her cast iron Dutch oven. Jeannette Goerdt's family likes to end their trips with "campfire pies" made of pie filling sandwiched between two slices of buttered bread cooked in a pie iron and topped with a dusting of powdered sugar.

S'mores, the classic campfire combination of toasted marshmallows and squares of chocolate sandwiched between graham crackers, are easy and fun to make. Olson's family has a different summer tradition; they layer peanut butter and white chocolate between Fudge Stripe cookies or chocolate or cinnamon graham crackers. Families that crave something different might like to try Banana Boats, the Walker family's favorite campfire treat. For each boat, simply peel back a single strip of banana peel leaving it attached at one end, and scoop out a bit of the fruit. Fill with chocolate chips and mini marshmallows, re-cover with the strip of peel, and wrap in foil. Throw into the fire for seven or eight minutes to melt all the goodies, then serve the boats right in their peels.

Most of us associate barbecues with late lunches or early dinners, but for Sandy Smith Hay, who grew up in Florida, the most memorable cookouts of all took place at an hour when most folks were still sleeping. The delicious bacon-and-egg breakfasts her parents cooked on a camp stove at the beach just after the first light of day were the highlight of the Smith family's summers for years. "We went before sunrise because of our fair skin," recalls Sandy. "It was so special, almost like Christmas morning. We would rise at five A.M. and put on our bathing suits. We would ride the causeway with the windows down and the bay breeze blowing in our faces. Once at the beach, we would unload and set up at *any* picnic table we wanted. The beach and the ocean were ours exclusively.

"The sun would just start to peek as we entered the water," Sandy continues. "Usually I was hanging on my father to keep above the waves, and the slight wind would make me shudder." The whole family stood in the water, watching the sun slowly light up the beach. They swam and played in the surf, then had breakfast. "By nine o'clock, as everyone else trudged through the sand to stake their claim on the beach, we were packing up to go home," Sandy says. "The beach and the sunrise had been ours and ours alone. I always felt we had the best of the day before nine." Either way—sunrise or sunset—plan to head for the beach with your family for a picnic breakfast or supper this summer. You'll be missing the crowds and the hottest part of the day, and you'll be giving your kids an adventure, as opposed to just another day at the beach.

Of course, you needn't leave your own backyard to make your family's summer meals special. A picnic table by the garden can transform any meal into a festive occasion, especially when you add an old quilt top for a tablecloth, a canning jar of Queen Anne's lace as a centerpiece, and some colorful tea towels as napkins. What better way to celebrate a summertime birthday! And if everyone lends a hand with food, chairs, and paper plates, it takes no time at all to turn a porch, patio, or deck into an outdoor dining room, which in turn can transform Wednesday night's leftover pork chops into a family picnic. For dessert you could try making your own ice cream, using fresh berries, peaches, or plums for flavoring. Serve with an array of toppings—sliced fruit, chocolate sauce, toasted coconut, crumbled cookies—and invite your family to make their own sundaes.

If you don't happen to own a set of sundae dishes, look for them at the yard or garage sales that are so plentiful this time of year. There you will find dozens of inexpensive items that can enliven your table all year long: wicker baskets for serving breads and rolls, wide-mouth earthenware crocks to hold cooking utensils for easy countertop access and storage; old quilts, runners, napkins, and cloths for your tabletop, and one-of-a-kind plates to display on your kitchen or dining room walls. Keep an eye out, too, for Depression glass, Fiestaware, enamelware, old china, and colorful pottery. Remember, for informal meals, dishes don't need to match; in fact, some of the most attractive settings for casual dining can be fashioned by combining complementary patterns or colors.

A wide variety of colorful dishes and table linens collected over the years can make mealtime much more fun, since any food looks more appetizing when it's beautifully presented. My mother-in-law, Maxine, swaps her everyday dishes twice a year, just to keep things interesting. Each October, she starts using her winter set: white plates with a nostalgic farm scene. Come April, those dishes go back into the basement and her summer ones, with delicate violets painted on them, are brought out. We always look forward to seeing those violets, for they're a sure sign that spring's on the way.

At their best, summer meals are fresh and colorful, casual and fun. But just as every day isn't sunny, neither is every meal special. As Shannon Werhanowicz says, "Our summer days often end with cranky kids who have had too much sun, no nap, and don't want to go to bed while it's still light out." I doubt there's a mother alive who hasn't found herself in that situation, since, for all its joys, summer also poses its fair share of challenges—including bored children with too much time on their hands.

Anything can get tedious when there's simply too much of it—even something as enjoyable as a summer vacation. So before Stacey Schrock's children have had a chance to even *think* about getting bored, Stacey helps them set up a card table under the shade tree in front of their farm for their favorite "school-is-out-and-summer-is-here" tradition: their annual summer "slush" sale. Along with fruit slushes and lemonade, Nathan and Rachel Schrock sell homemade cookies and mini-muffins to friends and neighbors for a couple of hours a day.

"What makes it so neat is that we live way out in the country—our nearest neighbors are a half-mile away and the closest McDonald's is twenty-five minutes away—yet people we know will go out of their way to stop by when they know the kids are going to have their sale," Stacey says. "It's a great excuse to stop whatever busy things we are doing and chat for a while. The kids glow when they tell us about who stopped and who gave them extra tips. It's definitely a summer highlight." And I suspect it's one the Schrock children will look back on with great fondness long after their childhoods end.

As Cindi Swett says, "It's funny. When I was growing up in my very small town I always dreamed while sitting in our canopy swing overlooking the mountain of coal of what it would be like to travel and be somewhere else. But now that I'm grown and have children of my own, I always find myself trying to re-create the little things that remind me of that very same small town."

I know just what she means. County fairs, ice cream socials, local strawberry festivals, and Sunday school

picnics—simple things that take me back to my roots—
are still among my favorite summer family activities. In
fact, one of my most enduring summer memories stems
from the annual potluck picnic my family attended at
our church many years ago. For the kids, there were
three-legged races, potato-sack races, ice cream, and
unlimited soda in bottles plucked from a wooden tub
filled with ice. There was also a water-balloon toss for
the adults in which my parents participated, laughing
and joking as they lobbed the balloon back and forth.
I'd never before seen them "play" with each other, and
the sight had a profound impact on me. For the first
time in my life, I saw my parents as individuals with
their own hopes and dreams, sorrows and joys, and this
split-second shift in perspective had a lasting positive
effect.

In our child-centered society, it is easy to lose sight of
the fact that we *all* need to take time to play. Those long,
lazy summer vacations we experienced as children may be
a thing of the past, but that isn't to say we can't recapture
the feeling that came over us on the last day of school, that
heady blend of anticipation, excitement, and happiness at
having our freedom restored. Nor should we adults over-
look the importance of balancing our own hectic lives.
This summer, just for the fun of it, remember to go out and
play. Toss a ball, savor a Popsicle, or run through a sprin-

kler or two. Summer's pleasures are as timeless as they are perishable, with a boundless capacity to revitalize and renew. Try not to miss a single one.

Family Reunions

It's a long journey from the southwestern corner of Missouri to the tiny town of Cimarron in western Kansas—particularly with seven people crammed into the car—but for Kelly Gibson, who made this ten-hour trip to her grandparents' with her family each summer, it was worth every hot, dusty mile. It was worth it for the typical Midwestern feast of roast turkey and stuffing, roast beef, mashed potatoes, green beans, and brown-and-serve rolls that awaited them upon their arrival; for the pranks Kelly's uncles delighted in pulling on her and her thirty-one cousins; for the thrill of seeing what improbable new combination of Jell-O, Cool Whip, marshmallows, and fruit Aunt Elsie, the resident "salad expert" of Texarkana, Arkansas, had concocted since the previous year.

"The meal was always preceded by prayer and thanking God for providing so bountifully for all of us," recalls Kelly, born thirty-two years ago into a family of ministers. "Then we filled our plates and headed downstairs. The cousins, once we were old enough, got to eat together in the main room in Grandma and Grandpa's basement. Eating was part of the fun, but we also enjoyed food fights and seeing how much corn we could throw into each other's Kool-Aid."

Once upon a time in America, family reunions didn't need to exist, because extended families tended to live near each other—often on the very street or on the same farm. Many lived their lives as single entities, eating meals together at the same table, enduring the same hardships, and weathering the same storms. They didn't have to come together on a yearly basis on borrowed folding chairs in Grandmother's basement, because they'd never really come apart.

For the vast majority of Americans, of course, that era is long gone. Nowadays, our so-called distant relations are distant in more ways than one, sprinkled across the country like sugar on pie crust. And while most of us do fairly well at keeping in touch with our immediate relatives, there's more to most families than parents, siblings, and grandparents. There also are uncles who pull quarters out of kids' ears and aunts who make great Jell-O salads.

My own extended family included my fun-loving Aunt Unabell, who pitched a tent on our lawn and made coffee over a campfire every time she came to visit our cottage in Michigan; my responsible Uncle Dave, who kindly monitored my education and sometimes accompanied my father to work to help him out; and my charming Uncle Mill, who, with his wife, Anna, kept horses on their Michigan farm. Of all my relatives, they were by far the most intriguing to me as a child, and the year we visited them and got to ride their horses was the most magical reunion of all.

There is something invaluable to be gained from virtually every reunion, though, for it is through our relationships with our extended families that we come to discover how and where we fit into the world. As Kelly Gibson says, "We never lived near family, and when your dad is a minister, while you have the congregation, you're never really a part of it." Nonetheless, she adds, "Mine is a very rich heritage, deeply rooted in Christian faith. All my uncles were ministers and all my aunts married ministers. Going to my grandma's house all those years gave me a true sense of identity and made me really grounded in my family."

That family includes its fair share of characters, like Kelly's fun-loving Uncle Leon. "'Let's pair up and smell armpits,' he used to say, and we little kids would just about die laughing," says Kelly. Later, the uncles would sing silly songs to the cousins, or unscrew all the lightbulbs and hide in the dark basement, springing out at the kids when they ventured downstairs.

For those of us like Kelly Gibson, details of those long-ago family gatherings loom large in our memory, right down to the bean pots and casserole dishes our aunts brought for potluck. We still recall how, on that one special day every year, our names were officially changed; instead of "Bonnie" or "Susan," we became "Sarah's oldest" or "Molly's youngest." At the same time, we learned that the features we'd thought of as uniquely our own were actually part of a set, as in "the Baker chin" or "the Sedgewick nose." An army of relatives eyeballed our growth, measured our baby fat, pinched our cheeks, and ruffled our hair. Having thus passed muster, we were free to run around with our cousins and stuff ourselves with desserts.

"There always seemed to be a breeze in the air, and the fragrance of flowers nearby," says Sandy Hay, whose family gathered in North Carolina. "The food was always delicious and homemade. When it came time to eat, the parade of potluck dishes was organized on the long table with military precision. The desserts came out first: pies, cakes, cookies, and sometimes a plate of fudge graced the end of the table. If you were smart, you never played far from that end." And if you were not only clever but resourceful, you made sure to stake an early claim to your favorites, lest another year go by without a taste of Martha's plum cake or Aunt Bertha's cherry pie.

Styles change, in food as in fashion, and some of those childhood favorites are dishes we no longer care to make. But the old family standards—lasagne and sauerbraten, stuffed cabbage and cheese enchiladas, raisin pie and strawberry-rhubarb—are often what hold us and our histories together, telling us all who we are and where we came from, marking us as kin as definitively as our curly hair, amber skin, hazel eyes, or slight overbite.

Coming together to prepare and share familiar foods helps families transcend the geographical distance between them. The recipes handed down from our mothers and grandmothers, on smudged and stained index cards faded with years, come to represent our collective, shared pasts, the roots from which all branches grow. No one knows this better than Pamela Etter, whose family gathered at the home of her grandmother to share food and fellowship on the Chesapeake Bay.

"There was always a ball game on the radio in the summertime," Pam says. "And there was always some kind of seafood. Steamed crabs in the summertime, oysters at Thanksgiving. Much of the time was spent around the table talking, as my grandmother was a very funny lady and always had a story to share. She thought her grandchildren were the most beautiful and smartest children on the face of the earth, so naturally, we loved being with her. And we loved her cooking. No one could make better crab soup or German potato salad—and that includes all the aunts on my dad's side!"

Such treasured recipes needn't be lost. When Muriel, the matriarch of the Nelsestuen family died, her relatives compiled her best-loved recipes into a cookbook as a memorial. "Some of the recipes were submitted by her children as their favorites, some were submitted by her longtime friends, some came from her ladies' group at the church," says Kelly Nelsestuen, who is married to Muriel's grandson.

The resulting cookbook, *Heart's Delight,* honors Muriel's

love of her family and the value of family meals. "After her death we made lots of copies, bound them, and gave them away—to those who knew her, to those who loved her, and to those who ate with her. It is such a joy for me to make the foods for my husband that he loved growing up and to prepare them as she did."

Not only do family cookbooks make wonderful tributes, they're also great gifts for friends and relatives, particularly new daughters-in-law or other newcomers. Don't wait for the matriarch of your family to compile yours. Simply ask the best cooks in your clan to send copies of their favorite recipes or bring them along to your family reunion.

Organizing such a get-together can be wonderfully rewarding, provided you start early and enlist everyone's help and support. The first order of business is deciding who should serve as the host—ideally, someone who's centrally located and who has enough time to help plan the festivities and enough space to accommodate everyone. But if you and your relatives happen to be short on both, there are other ways of divvying up the task.

In the Lucrezi family, for instance, six siblings take turns playing host to the one hundred or so family members who gather each summer in Lima, Pennsylvania. Only one sister, Margaret, has room for everyone on her small farm, so once every six years, the reunion is held there. The other gatherings are held at a local amusement park that features built-in entertainment in the form of rides and an old-fashioned penny arcade. My family gatherings often took place at picnic grounds, which offered plenty of tables and space.

If your extended family has outgrown its members' backyards, ask everyone to scout around for a suitable site, be it a fairground, a local church or synagogue, or a state park. When Melissa Stromberg's family expanded beyond the confines of her aunt's kitchen, their reunions were moved to the local senior center. Along with more space, the Strombergs gained several ovens and refrigerators, greatly simplifying the task of preparing and storing their family favorites.

Once you've agreed on a site, it's time to send out invitations, preferably several months in advance. Since invitations tend to set the tone for the gathering, think about the mood you wish to create as well as the foods and other items—extra folding chairs, for example—you'd like your relatives to bring. And consider asking for a small donation—the Lucrezis contribute ten dollars per family—to cover the costs of paper products and other supplies.

Hearty Italian dishes—manicotti, eggplant Parmesan, homemade sausages, and polenta—are among the Lucrezi family's specialties; at one recent reunion, relatives counted more than a half-dozen versions of the same dish.

If your relatives tend to cook similarly, you may wish to ask everyone to label their creations with the chef's name, the way the Lucrezis do. That way, everyone will know whom to compliment—and whom to ask for the recipe.

For many people who hail from large, ethnic families, reunions offer a chance to reconnect not just with our relatives but with our roots. We do this in large part by sharing the dishes our grandparents and their parents brought to America from their native lands. If your family doesn't have a strong ethnic identity on which to draw, there are other ways of celebrating your bonds and enlivening the menu and mood in the process.

One method of adding meaning and richness to your reunion involves giving your gathering a theme that relates to some aspect of your family history. Play up the family business with invitations that pay tribute to your ancestors' occupation. Was your great-grandfather a farmer? Cut a border of blue denim or cotton gingham fabric with pinking shears and glue the border onto a small piece of cardboard announcing the time, date, and place for your gathering, and ask everyone to bring a dish representative of down-home farm cuisine. Was the patriarch of your family a fisherman? Stencil lobsters around the border of your invitation and fill in the appropriate details, including a request for dishes that feature the catch of the day. You can then cover the cardboard with an old fishnet stocking cut to fit.

A collage of your relatives' baby pictures taken from old photo albums and photocopied, or copies of sepia-toned wedding portraits of your great-grandparents make lovely invitations to reunions that celebrate the past. If you're lucky enough to have a copy of the menu that was served at their wedding, you might try asking relatives to help re-create it.

You may also wish to highlight foods that are indigenous to your part of the country. "My dad showed us at an early age how to cook lobsters and steamers on the beach," says Nancy Kelleher, whose reunions always took place at her Aunt Grace's cottage at Seabrook Beach, on New Hampshire's tiny strip of coastline.

"We would take turns with him getting the sea water and seaweed. The seaweed is essential to having a perfectly steamed lobster," says Nancy, who adds that to this day, not one of her five siblings will order lobsters in a restaurant because they never taste anywhere near as good.

Of course, you needn't hail from New England to create a "Down East" clambake of corn, lobster, steamers, and potatoes. Nor is it necessary to move to the Bayou to put together a New Orleans feast of gumbo, jambalaya, dirty rice, and bread pudding. If your gatherings could use a bit of culinary inspiration, try targeting some other part of the country and incorporating its cuisine into your theme.

Or, if your extended family is as scattered as mine, you may wish to ask everyone to bring some regional food from their home state to add interest to your buffet table: maple sugar candies from Vermont; cheddar cheese from Wisconsin; citrus fruits from Florida; fiery salsa from New Mexico; and so on. Let the resulting feast reflect and celebrate the country's diversity as well as the family's!

It doesn't take much to add an exotic new wrinkle to the same tried-and-true family favorites. The jewel-like pomegranates plucked from her Aunt Roma Ann's backyard were a highlight of Melissa Stromberg's reunions, while the younger members of the Lucrezi clan still relish the memory of the sweet, juicy pineapples their Aunt Angie shared with everyone following her trip to Hawaii—the perfect foil for the heavy Italian specialties served up by her relatives.

The Lucrezi kids looked forward to helping prepare for the reunion almost as much as the reunion itself. Enlist your children's help in the planning stage, and share relatives' pictures with them in advance, lest all those aunts and uncles seem like strangers when they stream through the door. When Debbie Braverman's son, Ben, was a preschooler, one of their favorite rituals involved sitting down on the sofa with the family photo albums. "As Ben turned the pages, I used to tell him little stories about his uncles, aunts, and cousins," says Debbie. "That way, when he finally met them, he warmed up to them that much more quickly."

If you have lots of little ones in your family, consider hiring a professional to keep them entertained at your gathering: a clown who fashions animals out of balloons; a preschool teacher or day care provider with a vast repertoire of songs, games, and stories; an artist who does face painting; a local stable owner who gives pony rides. That way, adults who would otherwise spend the day chasing after their children will be free to sit down and visit with each other.

You may also wish to consider planning some type of

entertainment for grown-ups, letting your relatives' unique talents and interests play a role. "My husband's mother comes from a German family with fourteen siblings," Judy Rudenick says. "Being such a large family and being that they were raised during the Depression, they are quite close. The best part is that they are very musical and several play instruments, so the Hammerschmidt reunions are full of music, polkas, singing, and dancing." Background music adds to the ambiance of any party, so bring along a cassette or CD player and some tapes or disks. Zydeco complements jambalaya, Irish jig music goes nicely with corned beef and soda bread, and reggae lends an air of authenticity to Jamaican jerk chicken and barbecued shrimp, so use your imagination and choose music appropriate to your theme.

In putting together your program, ask yourself what your relatives have in common besides genes. Have everyone bring the appropriate supplies for some group activity: tennis racquets or a croquet set for a family tournament, individual squares for an heirloom quilt, film and cameras for an album of candid snapshots recording your good times together, or sturdy walking shoes for a family hike.

The setting for your reunion may also suggest an activity, such as building sand castles and swimming at a local beach. Sometimes we needn't look any further than our own backyards to find an entertaining diversion. After all, to my sisters and me, our uncle's farm was as exotic a "theme park" as Disneyland!

Cindi Swett's family never gathered without fistfuls of pennies for the mean poker games that were a fixture at their reunions. And giant watermelons were always de rigueur at Pamela Etter's family gatherings, for the seed-spitting contests held after the meal. The sheer informality of these gatherings is one reason they tend to be so much fun, so don't stand on ceremony, and don't hesitate to create your own silly traditions. Along with good food, there's nothing like lots of laughter to bring families closer together.

As with most informal gatherings, simple and casual tends to work best when bringing your kinfolk together, so save your good china and fancy tablecloths for some other day. As Nancy Kelleher says of her family's lobster feasts, "The tables were all different kinds from the neighborhood, covered with mismatched cloths held down with rocks. But you know what? It didn't matter to anyone that we ate on paper plates. We were together."

If the idea of a paper tablecloth strikes you as unacceptable, purchase some inexpensive flannel-backed material from a fabric store, along with a set of permanent pens. Write the year in the center, and let each person write his or her name and a few comments about the reunion. As your family grows with each passing year, so will your collection of reunion tablecloths. Think of the fun you'll have rereading all your cloths at subsequent gatherings!

Along with paper products, don't hesitate to employ other labor-saving techniques, or to take whatever shortcuts you can, since time with your relatives is the most important ingredient in any successful reunion. Whenever possible, think "self-service." Serve meals buffet style. Fill an old washtub with ice cubes and drinks. Wrap individual sets of plastic utensils in ribbon-tied napkins and stand upright in baskets at either end of the table, so everyone can just grab and go. Place several trash cans with plastic liners at strategic spots to greatly cut down on the cleanup.

In most places these days, banquet tables and folding chairs can be rented easily and inexpensively. Tie colorful balloons to the backs of the chairs to designate the children's table. Cover the surface with white butcher paper and place glasses of crayons within reach to keep little ones occupied while grown-ups chat. You may wish to place small "table gifts" at each setting. Yo-yo's, candies, or other age-appropriate items in brightly gift-wrapped boxes to be opened and enjoyed after dinner can go a long way toward keeping young kids entertained.

Scout summer yard sales in your area for attractive but inexpensive baskets that can be decorated with ribbons and placed on the tables ahead of time. Filled with fruit or wildflowers, the baskets make colorful centerpieces during the meal and handy containers afterward. Give one to each family, and let everyone browse the buffet table to select their own leftovers to take home.

A watermelon "basket" also makes a beautiful centerpiece that can be filled with fruit salad to be enjoyed after the meal. Using a serrated knife, cut a watermelon in half lengthwise, leaving a strip of rind in the center to serve as the handle. Hollow out the melon, reserving the fruit for the salad; for a fancier look, you can cut the edge of the rind into a scallop or zigzag pattern. Fill the empty basket with assorted fruits cut into bite-size pieces, and garnish with mint sprigs. Along with a colorful table-topper, you'll have a healthy alternative to the usual high-calorie sweets, one that's bound to be appreciated by relatives whose health problems make cakes, pies, and cookies off-limits.

A disposable camera is a great item to place on each table before guests arrive. "Pass it around, and give everyone a chance to take a picture of whomever or whatever they wish," suggests Sandy Hay, who finds the cameras to be wonderful icebreakers that invariably result in some great candid shots. A video camera is indispensable for capturing the flavor of your reunion. Wander from table to table while people are eating, and ask everyone to say a few words. The resulting tape can be copied and shared among relatives, or sent to family members who, for whatever reason, were unable to attend.

Recording elderly relatives retelling favorite stories—perhaps with grandchildren or nieces and nephews comfortably ensconced on their laps—is a great use of videotape as well, for it enables you to preserve a bit of your precious family history for posterity.

Another way to safeguard the past is by creating a family journal, which can be as simple as a loose-leaf notebook or as elaborate as a beautifully leather-bound book engraved with the family's surname. Pass it around, asking each person to record his impressions of the reunion or to share some memorable experience from the previous year, anything from the birth of a child to the passing of a loved one. When the pages are full, make copies for each family and start a new volume. Signed and dated, these books will become treasure troves of family history that can be excerpted and quoted for years to come, providing priceless material for everything from wedding toasts to eulogies to momentous birthday celebrations, not to mention free entertainment for all the reunions to come.

Amid all the festivities, be sure to set aside time for an official family portrait. Set up a tripod or ask a neighbor or friend to serve as your photographer, so that everyone gets in the picture. The resulting shots can be blown up and framed as holiday gifts, laminated and used as place mats, or reproduced on T-shirts to be proudly worn to the following year's get-together.

While most of us tend to schedule our gatherings during the summer, it bears mentioning that reunions needn't be limited to July or August. Take advantage of off-season rates to get together during the spring or fall months. Or plan a reunion to coincide with Thanksgiving the way the Sadwin family always does, alternating between Arnold's house in New Jersey and his sister Thelma's in New Hampshire. Christmas is another convenient time for a family gathering, when everyone's children have time off from school. Should you choose a December reunion, ask each family to bring a few treasured ornaments and decorate your spruce, pine, or fir all together, designating the finished product as your official "Family Tree."

One of the most unique gatherings I've ever heard of takes place on Mother's Day, when Nancy Belda and her seven sisters enjoy a special brunch prepared and served by their husbands. These brunches started out as elegant affairs held on Nancy's mother's patio, with her Waterford crystal and Belleek china. But somehow, over time, they devolved into hilarious "theme" brunches that the sisters enjoy even more.

They knew something was up the year they arrived at their mother's to find her normally manicured front lawn strewn with crushed beer cans. "All the men were dressed in jeans and bib overalls with straw hats on their heads," Nancy recalls. "My mom's garage door was raised to reveal hay on the floor, baled hay with a scarecrow, a table covered with a woolen blanket, a 'weed' centerpiece and pie tins for plates. Hillbilly music played in the background as the 'waiters' served us grits, bacon, coffee cake, and other goodies. They even danced with each other. We laughed ourselves silly."

The so-called "Hee-Haw" brunch was so well received that the husbands followed up the next year with a "Men at Work" theme featuring "waiters" in hard hats, simulated construction sounds, and a flower-filled toilet plunger as the centerpiece! The sisters have since been treated to a "Titanic" brunch complete with individual kickboards as place mats, waiters dressed as ship's mates and Goldfish crackers strewn on the table, along with a real, live goldfish in a bowl. Needless to say, "We eagerly look forward to Mother's Day and are constantly surprised by their creativity and attention to detail," Nancy says.

Sad to say, there are those of us whose extended families are simply too scattered or whose schedules are too hectic to make annual gatherings feasible at any time of the year. But we can still share our lives with our loved ones, albeit long-distance, by creating a family newsletter, taking turns assuming the role of editor in much the same way other families alternate hosting duties.

Family newsletters take time to produce, but the results can be well worth the effort. The layout can and should vary from editor to editor, but generally speaking, each newsletter should contain updates on every family, along with listings of births, job promotions, graduations, new addresses, and other milestones large and small. Obituaries, photographs, recipes, and features round out the copy, which can be easily assembled and reproduced using a laptop computer and basic software.

For most of the rest of us, of course, the real challenge isn't so much getting our families together once a year as it is maintaining contact between reunions. But if more and more of us tend to live far from our families, the good news is that our options for keeping in touch have never been greater.

Conference calls allow everyone to chat on the phone at the same time, and electronic mail makes written communication easy and instantaneous. Judy Black and her family have been communicating via e-mail for some time, and all find the results very satisfying. "Every Sunday, Grandma sits down at the computer and writes what has been happening and we all try to do the same thing," Judy says. "Even if you don't have time to write much, you still feel closer when you receive a 'letter' from your brother and sister."

For the more computer-literate, family web sites enable us to post news and photographs for all to see, while taking advantage of our children's affinity for high-tech options. Along similar lines, video newsletters are fun and easy to create, and can be mailed from household to household, with each family adding their own greeting at the end.

And overnight delivery services make it possible to send even the most perishable foods to our loved ones, for a welcome taste of home between visits. Each Thanksgiving, Cindi Swett eagerly awaits the arrival of a nut roll from her sister-in-law in Pennsylvania. Lobsters from New England, smoked salmon from Washington state, and steaks from the Midwest make wonderful gifts, as do homemade pickles, relishes, cookies, and cakes.

To keep that family feeling alive all year round, consider decorating the walls of your kitchen with beautifully framed photographs of your mother, sister, and grandmother in their own kitchens. Try your hand at re-creating one of their specialties, and keep them posted on how it turns out. You might even try organizing a long-distance "reunion" in which everyone prepares the same menu of family favorites in their own kitchens on the same day.

However you choose to keep in touch with your far-flung relations, make closer ties with extended family a priority for *your* family, for all the benefits and joys that they bring. Open up your home and heart to your aunts, uncles, cousins, and in-laws. Your life—and the lives of your loved ones—will be that much richer for having been shared.

Reaching Out

I've always made it a point to respect others' privacy, but I must confess to the following lapse: whenever I drive past a house at night and see people seated around the table, I can't help but pause for a moment to look in. The sight never fails to make me happy, for it speaks to me of nurturing, caring, and a sense of community. The people inside aren't always eating; sometimes I'll see them at the table and know at a glance it isn't dinner that has brought them together. Maybe they're playing a card game, piecing a jigsaw puzzle, or having a family discussion. Or perhaps they are trying to resolve a conflict that has somehow affected them all.

If so, I believe they've come to the right place, for I'd be willing to bet that more problems are solved at the table than anywhere else in the home. I'm not entirely sure why this is, but I suspect it has something to do with the positive feelings we bring with us each time we sit down together. Our memories of the good times we've shared—to say nothing of all that good food—help us make our way over life's inevitable rough spots. So Barb Wilson and her mother-in-law discovered, over a series of dinners that changed both their lives.

When Barb and her husband, Stuart, reconciled after a separation of nearly two years, Barb's happiness was tempered by worries that her relationship with her mother-in-law might never recover. "She was a close friend and during the separation, she had really cut all ties with me," Barb says. "Stuart's mom was very angry at the choices I had made and all the hurt I had caused her and the family. She didn't want anything to do with me because she was still hurt and didn't trust me. It was a very hard situation."

As the months passed, and her marriage grew stronger, Barb struggled to find common ground with her mother-in-law, an outstanding cook. Barb, on the other hand, wasn't known for her brilliance in the kitchen. "I was never asked to bring food to family gatherings," she says wryly, "other than the olives." Nonetheless, the next time the family got together, Barb decided to forgo the olives and attempt a new recipe, her mother-in-law's potato-cheese casserole. "That raised some eyebrows," Barb says. "Nothing much was said, but it felt so good to participate and contribute that I decided to try it again."

And so, when Stuart's grandfather came for a visit, Barb arrived at her mother-in-law's laden with offerings: a Vermont cheese dip served with star-shaped bread slices, a giant brownie "pizza" with a lemony filling and fresh berries on top, ingredients for assorted fruit ices the kids could create with Barb's help. "I figured if I worked in the kitchen all day with her, my mother-in-law would *have* to talk to me," Barb says. Her strategy seemed to be working; by day's end, she detected "a slight warming trend."

After that, Barb started bringing a new dish to her mother-in-law's whenever the opportunity arose. "I got more aggressive about helping clean up and serve," Barb recalls. "I was trying so hard to prove my intentions were sincere. My mother-in-law finally started to thaw."

Over the next couple of months, Barb continues, "We talked about food, we ate lots of it, we laughed, and we cried. It took time for the rift between us to heal, but I know in my heart it was those wonderful family recipes that helped bring us all back together. Back from the pain and hurt to the dinner table, eating, laughing, and building new memories together."

Food fuels our bodies, but the meals that we share can do infinitely more than that. They help ease our hurts and mend our fences; they foster connections we feared we had lost. Not just for a young wife temporarily estranged from her mother-in-law, but for anyone striving to find common ground. Just as we come to the table to celebrate the good things in life, so do we gather our loved ones around it during times of misfortune and loss: When a parent dies and we meet with our siblings to make the arrangements and give voice to our grief. When our closest friend suddenly loses her job and the bulk of her confidence along with it. When small disagreements escalate into big ones that require immediate action. I've often wondered what homing instinct leads us back to the table when events in our lives go awry. Perhaps it's the place where we feel the most grounded, and where we derive the most strength. Or maybe it's something more basic than that. Because sooner or later, we always get hungry. No matter what happens, we still need to eat.

But needing to isn't the same thing as wanting to, and we all have times when the difficulties we face threaten to tie knots in our stomachs and tighten our throats. We know we should eat, but unless someone's there to coax us, we find it easier somehow not to bother. Take Suzie Peterson, for example. When her father was being treated for cancer, Suzie found herself spending her mealtimes in hospital cafeterias surrounded by uneaten food—that is, until an old friend from high school came to her rescue. "In addition to keeping my family and me in her thoughts and prayers, she drove out just to share dinner with me so that I could get away and venture into the outside world," Suzie says. "Just eating a sandwich and talking about what was going on, the pain involved, and the things we've done to-gether in the past, turned out to be such a marvelous thing. Sitting at the table, it felt like I had been gone from the hospital for hours, but it had really been only forty-five minutes. It's the comfort of a true friend sharing a meal that can do so much healing."

If you have a friend in a similar situation and you find yourself wishing there were something you could do, re-member: there is something. Meet her for dinner and be there to listen, or to offer a change of scenery and a respite from her worries. If the patient's condition allows, you might also try bringing food to the hospital that all of you can sit and share. When Nancy Berns's father-in-law was hospitalized for an extended period, Nancy packed up grilled salmon, butternut squash, and some of his other favorites and brought them to him for his dinner. "Not only was he glad to have company," Nancy says, "but not surprisingly, he always ate much more of my cooking than he did of the hospital food. And it made me feel better knowing how much he enjoyed his special meals." The same holds true for nursing home patients, the elderly, or anyone living alone. Be sure to bring enough food so that you can join them, since having someone to eat with always makes everything taste that much better.

Of course, no discussion about reaching out to our families and friends would be complete without mentioning the importance of reaching out to those beyond our immediate circles. The family down the street whose breadwinner has been laid off; the folks across town whose child is battling a major illness; the people who've lost their home and belongings to a natural disaster. Each of us has a responsibility to those members of our communities who, for one reason or another, are experiencing hard times.

Many of us contribute to worthy causes throughout our workplaces, and I'm proud to say that my company, The Pampered Chef, is the largest cash donor to Second Harvest, the biggest hunger relief effort in the nation. More than that, our fund-raising efforts have helped bring my work colleagues closer together, as we rally together each year in support of this worthy cause. You may wish to launch a similar effort at your workplace or place of worship if no such program exists. Ask co-workers to help put together food baskets for less fortunate families in your area. It only takes one person to get a relief effort under way, and the results can yield big dividends for your community as well as your work "family." We all have an obligation as individuals to lend a hand to people in need. Each of us has something to give. As I am reminded so often by the kind efforts of my mother-in-law, Maxine Christopher, the most valuable commodity of all is our time.

Maxine has been preparing and serving dinner in a low-income, Uptown neighborhood of Chicago for as long as our family can remember. At least twice a year, she gathers together a group of twenty or so members of our church to travel to the Chicago Uptown Ministry to cook, serve, and entertain fifty neighborhood residents. Maxine has always been known for her wonderful cooking, especially by the folks at Uptown. Over the years, she and her helpers have prepared thousands of servings of turkey or chicken, mashed potatoes with gravy, and cooked carrots with dill, followed by warm pie or home-baked cake.

Helping Maxine produce and serve these special meals

has proven to be a rewarding experience for my family, one we look forward to year after year. If you've never lent a hand at a food bank or soup kitchen, I urge you to become involved. With each of us helping, we'll one day create a society in which everyone is assured of a place at the table—a table at which happy memories can be made.

Just as I never roast chicken and prepare gravy without thinking of my mother-in-law, most of us have certain dishes we strongly associate with our loved ones; our grandmother's pierogi, our great-aunt's apple fritters, our mother's macaroni and cheese. Taking the time to learn how to prepare your relatives' signature specialties can go a long way toward keeping their spirits alive after they're no longer with us.

When Becky Fudge met and married her husband, for example, her mother-in-law was ill with cancer. "She was a fighter and had a strong spirit, but all the time I was getting to know her, I couldn't help but think that someday, her fight might be over. I made it a point to learn all the special recipes my mother-in-law would prepare, like the biscuits and gravy she made for her sons when they would come to visit. I watched her and learned her secrets. My father-in-law traveled a lot, and when he would come home from a trip, she would have fried chicken, mashed potatoes, and gravy that night for dinner. I had her teach me how to make it so I could continue the tradition."

In December of 1996, Becky's mother-in-law went into the hospital, where she suffered a stroke and was placed on life support. "To say the least, the family was overwhelmed. That night for dinner, I made fried chicken, mashed potatoes, and gravy. No one said anything, but we all knew Peggy was with us when we had our dinner that night." Similarly, when Nancy Kelleher's beloved Aunt Grace passed away, Nancy created a special raspberry-chocolate torte for her wake. "Raspberries were Auntie Grace's favorite. And Auntie Grace believed you should have a piece of chocolate every day. She always had Russell Stover chocolates in her fridge, and she always ate one a day. I'm happy that I found a recipe that gave her both fruit and chocolate. She was there in spirit."

More than twenty years have passed since Barb Wilson last had dinner at her grandmother's house, but Barb still longs to sit down at that table. "Grandma Sennet died days before her first grandchild was born, but I still remember the smells in her house," Barb says. "I still remember her lumpy but fluffy mashed potatoes and warm applesauce. The jokes around the dinner table and the wonderful desserts. . . . I miss her so much, but eating those same foods and feeling fond memories is as comforting as 'comfort food' can be."

There's something inherently comforting, too, about the ritual of food preparation; the rhythm of the knife on the chopping block, the butter sizzling away in the pan. As Susan Allshouse discovered recently, these everyday sights and sounds serve as reassuring reminders that life goes on even during tough times. "My friend Denise's father was dying, and she had been taking care of him in her home. He was going downhill and I didn't know what to do," says Susan, who discussed her dilemma with her minister. "I told him I was sort of afraid to infringe on things right then. He explained that I should be there for her and that the best thing to do was to go to the store and get some food and other items she might need so that she had things on hand.

"Three of us went to the store and shopped for things we thought she might need," Susan says. "We got deli meats and buns, fresh produce, Kleenex, toilet paper, lotion, and so forth. We arrived unannounced and found Denise resting. We were able to make a meal for the hospice worker and for Denise, who woke up shortly after our arrival. We all ate together around the table. Denise talked about her father, and we were there to listen, to cry with her and to just be her friends. We stayed awhile and managed to get upstairs to clean her bathrooms, make up beds with fresh linens, and tidy up. Denise's dad died the next morning, and I was so glad I could do something to help a friend during one of the most difficult times in her life. Had it not been for food, that experience might never have happened. Denise still talks about that day. It meant so much to her and to all of us."

Likewise, when a close family friend of Lisa Walker's lay dying at home, Lisa searched for a way to be helpful. "Many people were coming to visit, in and out all day. There wasn't anything to do but sit and talk, cry, and remember his life. I couldn't take the stillness and decided to cook something. Maybe the smell of the food would be a comfort to Harry and everyone else around. I went to the grocery store and picked up a variety of things. I decided to concoct some potato soup. This gave a few of us an opportunity to busy ourselves peeling and dicing. Not only were we able to occupy our time, but we found it therapeutic to be preparing a nourishing pot of soup that smelled inviting and comforting. Whenever we talk of that day, we all remember what a great thing it was to do."

Having recently lost her grandmother, Stacey Schrock agrees. "I had friends and neighbors who stepped in and took care of our food for a couple of days. I had taken meals to people at different times, but I never realized until now what a blessing that food can be. The comfort it brought to see people bring dishes in was amazing to me," Stacey says. "We would have had food to eat—it's not like we would have starved—but the caring behind the food meant more than the food itself. It also made me realize how much a tray of cookies or an apple crisp can mean to someone, just to let them know someone is thinking of them and cares."

You may wish to coordinate your cooking efforts with those of neighbors and friends, so that everything doesn't arrive all at once. Most people need help feeding relatives and out-of-town friends attending the funeral of a loved one. But in the aftermath of a loss, families sometimes find themselves overwhelmed by the sheer volume of food friends bring over—so much so that they run out of storage space and end up having to give food away. Depending upon the situation, you may want to wait a few days before contributing. By this time, your friends undoubtedly still won't feel like cooking, and they may well have run out of supplies. They may also be ready to venture out for a bit, so you might try inviting them over for dinner. You can always bring the meal to them if they decline.

However you choose to proceed, don't let feelings of awkwardness or fear of intrusion stop you from making this most loving of gestures. Taire Render belongs to a group of women who make and deliver meals to fellow members of their congregation in times of loss. "I have been on both the receiving and giving end of those meals. Sometimes I think we take them for granted, but then I will hear someone say, 'My dad died and I felt so alone. No one brought food or anything.' It is then that I realize how important this gesture is. There are times when our souls are hungry and thirsty and need to be fed. During these days, I think, it is vitally important to feed our bodies, that they might be strong in order for healing to begin."

When Louise Swett died in Daytona Beach, Florida, just after her ninety-second birthday, her family's hearts began healing immediately, thanks to the instructions Louise left behind. The funeral was scheduled for a beautiful day in December, and Swetts from all over the country had flown in to pay their respects to the elegant matriarch of the family, recalls Cindi Swett, who is married to Louise's grandson. As it happened, Louise had very specific ideas about how she wished for her family to say their good-byes.

"Louise wanted to take one last ride on the beach, and she wanted us to feed the seagulls. We were all in three white limousines behind the white hearse—the grand-daughters and their mothers in one, the grandsons and their fathers in another, the other relatives in the third— and we had twenty bags of bread among us," Cindi says. "And so, with a police escort, we all rode on the beach with hundreds, maybe thousands, of white seagulls follow-ing." It was an arresting sight, so much so that even the tourists took note.

In lieu of presents for her birthday that year, Louise had requested that original artwork be drawn for her by her grandchildren and great-grandchildren. She never got to see all the drawings, paintings, and mobiles they made her, but her mourners did. "Instead of flowers, the pictures, drawings, and mobiles hung all over her casket, inside and out. It was beautiful," Cindi says. "It turned a very sad oc-casion into a memory that still brings a smile, something we'll always remember."

That night, following Louise's instructions, the whole family gathered at her favorite restaurant for a dinner cele-brating her long, happy life. "It was a bittersweet time, but when the memories started flowing, love and laughter soon followed as we shared our meal," Cindi says. "There was no doubt in our minds she was with us."

Sometimes it's the simplest meals that end up mean-

ing the most, as opposed to the elaborate ones. For instance, the most memorable dinner of Nancy Kelleher's
life was one that she watched her big sister, Lainie, struggle to sip through a straw. It was Lainie's first meal at
home with her family after spending six months in the
hospital, recovering from a near-fatal car accident that
had left her with more than a hundred fractures in her
face alone. Today, Lainie is alive and well, with a wonderful husband and two beautiful daughters. As Nancy
says, "Her face may look different, but thank God, she
has the same strong, good heart."

As Nancy's story reminds us, there are all kinds of losses
to be endured in this life. Some are inevitable, but others
can be avoided if we maintain our perspective about what
really matters the most. So Susan Terray concluded when
her father died recently, four years after the death of her
mom. After the funeral, Susan and her siblings sorted
through her father's belongings in preparation for selling
his house. Eventually, there remained just one task, one
that all four of his kids had been dreading. They needed to
divvy up the possessions that hadn't been addressed in the
will: the china, the silver, the crystal.

"All my life, I've heard horror stories about families
fighting over stuff like this," Susan says. "I desperately
didn't want that to happen." And it didn't, thanks in part
to the family table, where the final disbursement took

place. "We piled everything on the kitchen table, and we pulled our chairs up to the corners, each of us taking deep breaths," Susan says. "Someone found an old bottle of sherry and four little glasses, and we drank a toast first to our mom and pop. Then we went around the table, taking turns choosing items. To help keep things light, my brother, Robin, turned it into 'Let's Make a Deal.' 'Will she choose the gold china? No! She's going for the teapot instead!'

"So many of the items evoked such strong memories," Susan continues. "The metal dish Mom always used when she put the celery in the refrigerator . . . All four of us looked at that dish and said, 'Celery!' The silver creamer. The plates. That it happened at the table made it easier to do. It took what could have been a horrible situation and made it bearable. And afterward, we went out and had dinner together. Mom and Pop would have been proud."

Timeless rituals in familiar settings help us cope with all manner of losses even as they remind us to get on with our lives. So go ahead: Put a box of chocolates in your refrigerator and eat one—just one—every day. Keep the good silver creamer displayed on your table, not just on holidays but every day. Spend one Sunday a month serving those who are less fortunate. Make your mother-in-law's biscuits and whenever you serve them, lift your glass in a toast to her memory. Appropriate the table rituals of the people you love. Cherish their legacies, celebrate their lives, and keep them, forever young, in your heart.

Epilogue

O ver the coming year, the majority of us will probably consume somewhere in the neighborhood of a thousand meals—everything from breakfast bagels eaten on the run to the occasional multi-course dinner. Most likely, we'll eat roughly half these meals by ourselves, while doing paperwork at our desks, say, or catching the seven-forty-two express to the city. We'll skip a few breakfasts, all the while knowing we shouldn't, and pick at countless luncheon salads during corporate meetings. There'll be the occasional ball park hot dog, movie popcorn, or shopping mall burger. Now and then, we'll have brunch with a friend.

That will leave perhaps two or three hundred "family meals," from bowls of cereal silently gobbled at dawn to Friday night pizzas (delivered); from peanut-butter-and-jelly sandwiches served as after-school snacks to the turkeys on our Thanksgiving tables. The moods, like the menus, will no doubt run the gamut, from the giddy excitement of the first day of vacation to the mind-numbing bickering that accompanies too much rain. We'll experience the contagious silliness that erupts at the end of a long week, as well as the sudden shyness that comes to the table with guests.

As is true of virtually everything we do with our families, all will not go according to plan. Beans will burn, milk will spill, and no one will care for the lentils. Children will, now and then, leave the table in tears, and so, once or twice, will their moms. And yet, for all that, there'll be moments of joy that will more than make up for the tears, moments that will live on in our mind's eye forever. Like the sight of our sleep-tousled children bundled up in their warm flannel robes, their mouths filled with hot pancakes and syrup on a freezing cold Sunday in March. Or the picture they'll make in their new holiday outfits, all impeccably neat, clean, and pressed, shampooed heads bowed for their grandfather's blessing.

There'll be a few special outings stored away in our memory banks: breakfast at the ocean, where we'll all watch the sunrise, just like the Smith family once did; a watermelon seed-spitting contest at our family reunion, like the ones Pamela Etter remembers; a clambake just like Nancy Kelleher's, complete with lobsters, sea water, and corn.

But if you're anything like me and my family, most of the meals you'll remember will be far less extraordinary than that, just random moments and fleeting images you'll replay again and again: The day your three-year-old made her first joke. That good talk you all had when the fish died. Your seven-year-old son's first attempt at beef stew.

Of course, you'll remember the birthdays: the look on your daughter's face when she sees the special cake you stayed up past midnight to bake, or the lump in your throat when you woke up to breakfast—and all three of your kids—in your bed. Those special Valentine cookies, the St. Patrick's Day dinner with green mashed potatoes, the Fourth of July sparklers in the blueberry pie. The hot fudge sundae party when your kid's soccer team won the championship. The neighborhood potluck on Halloween night.

And yet, it probably won't be the special occasions that will bring you the most joy of all. It will be the odd moments, the littlest things, that happen of their own accord. The spontaneous hug and kiss on a Wednesday. The unsolicited compliments on your Monday night roast. Your mother-in-law's request for the recipe for the crab dip you created yourself.

There'll be the cinnamon toast you'll share with your daughter on a blustery Monday when she's home with the flu. The candlelight dinner you'll share with your husband when your kids sleep at their grandparents' and your house seems too quiet. The Happy Meals you'll eat on a blanket in January in front of the fire while wearing your shorts.

As you sift through the moments, there'll be a handful of things that you'll find yourself able to track, like the steady improvement in your kids' table manners, or their progress at getting along. You'll remember your daughter's announcement (how could you not?) that from now on, she'll no longer eat meat. You'll recall the miraculous day your young vegetable phobic agrees to try "little trees" (a.k.a. broccoli) and decides—saints be praised!—that he likes them.

But there'll be no way to pinpoint which of those three hundred meals helped raise your kids' reading scores or improve their vocabularies. Nor will there be any way of knowing which ones taught them to take turns and be patient, or to eat wisely for long, healthy lives. At what breakfast did they finally acquire a strong enough sense of themselves to stand up to peer pressure? Over which dish of spaghetti and meatballs did they decide they trusted you enough to come to you for help with their problems?

And, for that matter, which of the countless plates of meatloaf kept you happily married while other people's marriages fell apart? Which Sunday dinner was it, exactly, when your mother and father transformed themselves into your friends? When you found yourself wishing your siblings lived closer, and that your grandparents could live forever?

Those are but a few of the questions you'll never be able to answer. But here's one I'm hoping you can: Isn't it worth the investment of effort and time to summon your family to the table? Because the more times you do it, the better your odds of high reading scores, happy marriages, solid values, and bright, healthy kids. The ideas on these pages will help you get started; after that, it will be up to you. I hope this will be just the beginning, and that you and your loved ones will go on to create your own special rituals and celebrations, your own traditions and wonderful times.